FRANK N. D. BUCHMAN
Minister of Jesus Christ
in
Grateful Fellowship

Twice-Born Ministers

By

S. M. SHOEMAKER, Jr.
Rector of Calvary Church in New York

*"The real deliverance, the twice-born folk
insist, must be of universal application."*
—William James

Varieties of Religious Experience

TWICE-BORN MINISTERS

CONTENTS

" They were changed men themselves before they went about to change others."—WILLIAM PENN: *Preface to George Fox's Journal.*

" I went to America to convert the Indians; but oh, who shall convert me? . . . It is now two years and four months since I left my native country in order to teach the Georgian Indians the nature of Christianity; but what have I learned myself in the meantime? Why, what I the least of all suspected; that I who went to America to convert others was never myself converted to God."—JOHN WESLEY: *The Journal.*

"All the faithful are not called to the public ministry; but whoever are, are called to minister of that which they have tasted and handled spiritually."—JOHN WOOLMAN: *The Journal.*

" It seems to me that conversion and the new birth make the real attack today."—T. R. GLOVER: *in a Letter to the Author, August, 1927.*

" We need today ministers who take their work *seriously;* but this seriousness must concern itself for the *inwardness* of the Church and in no sense for the Church itself. The ministers who are concerned for the Church are no longer equal to the almost infinite seriousness of our present condition."—KARL BARTH: *The Word of God and the Word of Man.*

FOREWORD BY THE AUTHOR

I HAVE been thinking for some time about the possible usefulness of a book which might be written primarily, though not exclusively, to stir and deepen the spiritual life and enrich the practical service of ministers. During the past spring that idea grew " warm," and pieces of the book began coming to me with that curious, irresistible pressure, of writing which has to be done. It seems to me clear that the best way to help people concerning religion today is not only to present convincing, objective reasons to their minds, but also to show them pictures of those who are finding rich spiritual experiences, pictures which will rather fire their imaginations than persuade their minds. And so I wrote to upwards of a dozen of my friends, in whose lives I believe great spiritual happenings have been taking place, and asked them if they would join me in the venture of a book about " twice-born " ministers. They have given me the facts and the stories, and in most cases I have recast these into their present form. The book is theirs as much as mine, and I want to accord them at the outset my necessarily anonymous but none the less sincere thankfulness.

The first question which the book may raise lies, of course, in the title. Lest any one wonder at my use of a title so similar to that of the well-known book, *Twice-Born Men,* by the late Harold Begbie, let me say that I asked my friend Mr. Begbie, some months before his death, if he would consent to my use of the present title, and he cabled me in characteristic generosity, " Yes, certainly." I wish to acknowledge my debt to him for the spiritual stimulation of his many books, for the very idea of a book of brief spiritual biographies, for his friendship, and for this permission which was his latest kindness.

In replying to the obvious query, "Are not all ministers twice-born? " I should like first to define my terms a little. In " twice-born " I am using a term which was, I believe, made classical in William James' *Varieties of Religious Experience*. The term refers to the age-old experience of conversion, or rebirth. For a Christian, conversion ultimately means a complete experience of Jesus Christ; and the degree to which any of us is truly converted is measured by the likeness of our lives and our spiritual experiences to the lives and experiences of the disciples whom He so vitally touched when He was here among us in the flesh. Specifically, I feel that we have lost certain great experiences of the apostolic age—not lost them from our vocabulary, but lost them to a large extent from our lives. For the most part, I feel that we ministers are not putting within reach of our people the dynamic, transforming experience of conversion: we help many people, but we change few. Again, we believe generally in the direction of the Holy Spirit, preach about it, and some of us in the Episcopal Church pray often, in the words of one of our collects, that He " may in all things direct and rule our hearts:" but we seldom expect our people to reach the place where His guidance is an abiding possession, instead of an occasional surprise. Again, we talk a good deal in these days about evangelism, and from our pulpits we urge our people to " go out and share Christ with the world," but we are vague about how it can be done, and we are not surprised when it remains undone, and comfort ourselves with the thought that our people might have been tactless anyway if they had tried it.

All this produces as characteristic a singularly tame kind of religious experience in our people, an experience that is comforting and peace-giving but anæmic, sub-normal, and very different from its prototype of apostolic days. Sometimes when I hear a preacher reminding a comfortable congregation of Episcopalians of the apostolic nature of our Church, I want to say to him and to them that there is something else to apostolic Christianity beside historic derivation. There is apostolic enthusiasm, apostolic faith, and apostolic results. That kind of power is as accessible as it ever was. And we are none of us converted to Jesus Christ until we are finding it, and helping others to find in Him a living actuality for men and women today, delivering them from their fears and their sins, changing their hearts and their homes, making them happy, intelligent witnesses for Him, and putting upon their lives that indefinable but unmistakable mark of joy, assurance and power. I believe that the proof that a minister is twice-born lies not in compliance with any arbitrary prerequisite, but simply in the power to produce more twice-born people.

I feel that I must say something also to those who may feel that a book like this is somehow an " exposure," and will unseat the trust and loyalty of our people by showing them that ministers have the same kind of needs as themselves. There are two issues here: reverence for inward experiences, and the wisdom of telling about them generally. Some of these stories, as I read them fresh from the hearts of the men themselves, seemed to me to be written in blood: I read them with reverence, and I hope that others will do likewise. If anything on earth is sacred, it is a man's traffic with his God. It has been my privilege to help many of these men in their spiritual pilgrimages: and I will take second place to no man in my reverence for their personalities and my desire that their religious experiences should be regarded with seriousness and respect. But when any one recoils from an honest spiritual history, especially when anonymously presented, I think he needs to ask himself whether his recoil comes from a high and redemptive view of human life, with all its desperate needs, or whether it comes from too easy concession to his own squeamish tastes.

Have you ever stopped to ask yourself how we know about the Temptation of our Lord Jesus Christ? He was alone, for forty days: yet those three temptations are vividly recorded in two Gospels. The explanation must be that He told His disciples what had happened, and that they thought the whole world forever should know. Or Gethsemane—with the Son of God sweating drops like blood there under the trees, and His three intimates drowsy with sorrow and sleepiness—how do we know what happened? He must have told them afterwards, and they felt it no exposure that the holiest moment of struggle this world ever knew should be set down in books which multitudes should read. I think we may have pushed the business of reticence a little too far, in our desire to avoid excess and talkativeness, and made it the screen of a defective experience. Most people do not put their names on their doors; but doctors do, and you may call it advertisement if you will, but when your child has been hurt and you need help, that little sign exposed on the street is more welcome than a fortune. It is generally in the minds of people pleasantly remote from the more desperate of human need that one finds this unwillingness to give the uttermost of the innermost for the sake of others. As for such a book as this disturbing the trust of our people in their ministers, it is my opinion that some ministers have too long kept up the deceit that they have not the same problems as their people, that those who still entertain notions of our superior holiness are the aged, the spiritually dull and the " churchy," and that we had much better think a good deal more about the thousands outside our fold who will listen to us with much more patience the nearer we begin to their own situation.

It will be seen, I think, before the reader has gone very far, that the kind of work which we are describing lies much closer to the intelligent, patient sympathy and fact-finding of the psychiatrist than to the hasty, emotional and fact-ignoring exhortations of the worse type of evangelist. Many, indeed most, of the ministers in this book are settled in regular charges, where zeal without knowledge would very soon return to damage their work and their influence.

A movement such as is represented by these stories is likely to go through two successive stages of estimate at the hands of the people concerned for religion. The first shows itself in remarks like this: " The movement is an innovation. It is not scriptural. It is contrary to the genius of the Church. It is full of

danger." As more and more lives find Christ through
the movement, these arguments seem less and less
valid. The second may be much more sinister, for
all its acquiescence, " This is only just what we have
always believed. I have been doing this all my life."
Perhaps you have. But are you sure you have?
How many men and women have you in your congregation to whom you can send a life in great need,
and be sure that that person will find in them a
radiant, intelligent witness to what Jesus Christ has
done for them, which they make contagious by their
own spiritual joy? How many people have you who
are watching out for spiritual chances all the time,
not spending all their effort on church-suppers and
fairs and sewing night-gowns for Esquimaux, but
quietly transforming lives and homes about them,
and making Christ a living power to others? *Many
ministers mistake sympathy with the idea for realization of the actuality.* There is a seminary professor who heartily endorses " individual work," yet
I know men and women who have gone to him for
help, and their needs have been utterly missed, though
his reception was cordial and his conversation brilliant. Not many men in the ministry know how to
dig out the real facts in people's lives, or expect them
to become workers of moral miracles in others, or
help them to see the issues involved in surrender to
Christ, and gently keep after them till they make
that surrender. Most of us are thoughtful, intelligent
and kind toward our people, but we do not expect
heroic results. The upshot is that we are leaving
people in the vestibule of Christian experience; their
religion is more an aspiration than a possession; and
the world thinks that this is all that Christ can do!

Now we often say that there is nothing new in this movement, and that is true: the ideas come from the New Testament, and all down the ages some people have known them and lived triumphantly by them. I think that I remember seeing somewhere that Phillips Brooks once wrote a tiny note in his diary which said " Problem: to turn intellectual perceptions into life." I doubt if there is an idea in this book which is unfamiliar to any minister who reads it: but the incarnation of those ideas in transformed lives, and in a transformed parish, may be less familiar.

It is my hope that this book may be of some help to lay-people also. First in understanding that we parsons are much more like them than we may seem over a pulpit, that we need their patience and their help, as well as their loyalty and their support. But, deeper than this, there is many a spiritual layman who wonders why his parish drags so, why there is so much worry and talk about money, why the sheep look up and are not fed. We have moved far past the day when the laity took us for granted. Many of them respect our office who have little use for ourselves. Many whom we have thought to win by accommodating our principles, by making it all seem easier than it really is, and by going gingerly, would first believe in our sincerity if we spoke more plain truths, preached more about sin, and went after individuals with more courage. A layman came in to see me awhile ago and asked me to " prescribe for a sick church," and told me of the ineffectualness of his parson. I don't believe in letting any one confess other people's sins without confessing his own: I asked that man what he was doing beside reading the lessons when the parson's throat was tired, and helping with organizational details—was he winning anybody, was he alive himself, had he a contagious experience of Christ? But I felt all the time, also, that a parson with a dead spiritual life was back of much of the trouble. We have tamed most of our laymen: they are docile servants of the ecclesiastical machine. But now and again we find one who is restless and dissatisfied. I should like to say to such men that they do not always best serve their church by sitting still and keeping quiet—that they might occasionally serve it better by going, after much prayer, and saying out their hearts to their dominie, and talking with him honestly about the personal and spiritual causes of their church's failure, in the spirit of "Lord, is it I?" It is so easy in such a conversation to fall back upon secondary causes, such as want of money; but it is the continuing experience of some of us that where lives are being changed money does not lack. There is such an enormous lot that laymen can do in the matter of intelligent evangelism that I am in hopes that some of them will see themselves mirrored more than once in these stories of clergymen, discover a way out, and begin themselves to be fishers of men.

I believe that the Church today is in great need. Its outward prosperity was never greater: it owns more property, has more members, gives more for missions than ever in the past. It stands fairly well with the world—perhaps too well—as an institution which helps the community. Hundreds of rich men support it for no other reason than that without it vice, disorder and anarchy would increase: but it has nothing personally for them. The Church has lost the ear of the average man, who thinks it may be well enough for his wife, and his children while they are little; and it is meaning less than we like to think for the ordinary church-member. Go to the average service, and what earthly likelihood is there that people will come away materially different? In an immovable congregation, a man stands up to read from the New Testament, in a monotonous voice, words vibrant enough to wake the dead! But the sense has left them—they are today lovely literary music. Well, they weren't written to be " lovely literary music," they were written to bring life to human souls. How many sermons do more than throw a little light upon one aspect of Christian truth: how many of them go for the unsurrendered heart of a man and make him want to forsake his sins and help him to give himself decisively to God? No secondary devices are going to change all this. The Church needs a fresh impetus, one of those waves of spiritual refreshing which God has sent from time to time in history.

Where shall we get it? Sometimes one is a little appalled when he hears ministers talk about possible remedies. One declares for more religious education. And I want to say to him that I believe in religious education also, where it leads to religious experience in the children, where it shows them God's helpfulness in their own little problems and worries and helps them actually, one by one, to find God as their Friend: but that I have seen a good deal of a fact-purveying process which calls itself religious education, and I think it a miserable failure as generally conducted, and that only converted teachers with an experience of Christ can make Christ real to children, no matter how many normal classes they attend.

Another man says that his services are not beautiful enough, and he is doing over his church and installing a new organ and a system of delicate lights, and toning up his liturgy. And one wants to say to him that one believes in a thorough equipment and a beautiful church: but these noble auxiliaries to vital religion are not vital religion in themselves, many a parish house has been the mausoleum of a man's message, and the most beautiful Gothic interior in the world is only an expensive tragedy when it resounds with formal services and powerless sermons which do not really change lives. Another is going to give himself tirelessly to helping the humanity which comes to his door, broken, poor, unemployed people; and one thanks God for ministers who care about them and will give them time. Yet one wants to say to a man like this that he can find a needy man a job, or get a sick one to a doctor, or feed a hungry one, or encourage a despondent one, and he is only doing what a social case-worker could do better, and that if these processes do not include ultimately the experience of conversion to Christ, the personal factors in the situation may have been alleviated but they have not been cured: a minister of Christ ought to have no time for any human service which does not have as its ultimate object the winning of a life for Christ. So one might deal with the innumerable helpful things which can be suggested: more calling, more social gatherings, more congregational singing, more expository preaching—excellent suggestions all of them, but none of them profound enough to touch the root of the matter. I should consider that I had done any minister a service if I could help him to scrap these things as sufficient remedies for a dead church. They are too mild in the face of our need. Religion has lost its power to claim people's attention: what is the use in improving our means when they are not yet concerned about our ends? What we need is nothing less than spiritual revival.

And again I ask, Where shall we get it? Some years ago I was talking in London with the head of one of the theological colleges in Oxford, a man of wide reputation, great learning and shrewd common sense. He said that he did not know a dozen men in England to whom he could send a human soul in desperate need and searching for God. I asked him what he thought was the way out of such a state of things, and he said, " We must convert the parsons." This was not a quip, or a chance cynicism: it was the distilled judgment of a wise Christian leader. I have never forgotten his remedy.

Now I have been amazed at the number of ministers who are honest enough to realize, and humble enough to admit, that this great experience has never come to them, and who are looking for it wherever they can find it. I talk with a good many of them, and one hears from them constantly of the want of power and joy, of the failure to bring people definitely to Christ, of dissatisfaction and fear and worry and sin which spoil and weaken their ministry. It is no effort to put myself in their situation, and it is natural to tell them of my own powerless missionary service after college, during which I had no sufficient experience of Jesus Christ to be able to bring a Chinese schoolboy to discipleship; and then to go on and tell them how my meeting with Frank Buchman showed me conclusively that basic unsurrender in my own life was the problem, that I needed to be twice-born and never had been, for all my church-going, and what a joyous thing the ministry has been since the day when I " let go " one night in the West City of Peking, eleven years ago. Let me say here that I do not stand apart from the minister who needs to be twice-born: I am recommending to him a process through which I needed to pass myself, and I know full well that that process is still being worked out in my own life. But it is a great thing to feel that one has something to say to such a minister as wrote me only a few weeks ago, " For nearly two years I have been deeply interested in your work at Calvary Parish. I have read everything I could find, including your books and the Calvary Evangel. The conviction has been growing upon me that my own ministry lacks those essential qualities I have found in the work at Calvary. More than ever before I have been brought to a great sense of need in my own life, and that what is lacking in my ministry is really lacking in my life." Since that was written, he too has joined the happy ranks of " twice-born ministers."

I feel that the theological seminaries could help more than they do with their students. Many a man goes into the ministry, not because he has found, but because he is seeking: some have gone into it desperately hoping to find its fences high enough to keep some desires out of their lives. A belief that Jesus Christ is in some way bound up with the best we know, and a general desire to serve humanity through the Church, does not constitute a developed message, and may not have delivered a man from some of his own most elementary needs. For men who have not been converted before they enter a seminary, the experience of conversion ought to be made available for them while they are there. One sympathizes with the faculty's emphasis on studies, for one deplores an uneducated ministry: but studies have been getting all the attention of late years, and I submit that an unconverted ministry is as signal a tragedy as an uneducated ministry. One hears some stress laid upon the devotional life in the seminaries. But some men will never know how to pray or to make use of the sacraments till they have surrendered themselves to God: and it is useless to hammer away at small devotional habits when large areas of life are clear outside the domination of Christ. What men like this need is a very full, frank talk with an unshockable professor who will deal with them precisely as he would with a collegian, get to their basic problems, whether pride, dishonesty, lust or ambition, and bring them to a complete surrender of their lives. That will do more to tone up studies, and invigorate the devotional life of the seminary than anything else that can happen. When this is evaded, we are using mustard-plasters where radium or the knife are wanted. The real inwardness of many a minister's failure lies in a theological course which never touched him in the deep places of his life. It is an awful thing, after you have gotten into the ministry, to sit face to face with a man battling against the same sins as you have yourself, and to know that as a minister you must make hear-say recommendations, when as a man you cannot tell him of real victory through Jesus Christ. The deans and professors often say these things in sermons and chapel addresses, but it is one thing to recognize the need, another to meet it in the concrete and help a man out of it. No amount of theological or ecclesiastical information can make a servant of Christ's Church rich if his own soul is poor.

But happily, whether a man gives himself to Christ altogether before he is in seminary, or while he is there, or long after he gets out, it is never too late for a great experience to come to him which will transform him and his ministry and his church. One has seen these things come to men long past fifty. There is no reason for any discouraged, disappointed, unconverted minister to stay as he is. The failure of his church does not lie, I believe, in his want of personality or ability, or the peculiar indifference of the people in his community: it lies in himself, in his own want of profound consecration; the church fails because he lacks in himself the light of authentic inspiration. These things do not depend upon the accidents of age or personality or temperament or education or circumstances. "The difference between men," wrote Forbes Robinson, "is not that one is inspired and another is not, but that one yields to the Spirit, another does not."

I hope that it is unnecessary for me to say that no man in this book considers himself to have "arrived." Most of them would say, I think, that they know they are well started, in a sense in which they were never started before their surrender to Christ came. One is deeply sensible that the Christian life is a long road, for ministers as for everyone else, and that it is easy to take a wrong turning, or to get off the road entirely. We are not confusing what theologians call "regeneration" with "sanctification." We are only saying that through the experiences which have come to us there have opened up sources of power which

we had not tapped before, and that we have been
enabled to bring that power into the lives of others.
I think that it would be fair to say of all the men in
this book that they are very diffident about their own
spiritual progress, but also very sure about the truth
and reality of the message itself.

I should also like to say that I do not consider this
book to be the outcome alone of our work at Calvary
Church. The First Century Christian Fellowship is
now a movement of international proportions, and we
at Calvary are a part of it. With the experiences of
some of the men in this book I had personally nothing
to do. They came about by means of other members
of the Fellowship, some of them in other lands. I am
glad to be able through this book to pay a little of my
debt to the First Century Christian Fellowship, and
to record again my wholehearted and unconditional
identification with it.

Through this little book a dozen men in the ministry
are saying to you, whether you are minister or layman, that a great thing has happened to them which
can also happen to you—something which did not
destroy but fulfilled and enriched their former religious
convictions and experiences, which has helped them in
knowing how to meet people's deepest needs, and
freed them from innumerable burdens which they used
to carry. The deepest mark of reality upon these
stories, as I see them, is the radiant spiritual joy
which shines through them. It is only the truth that
makes men free.

S. M. S., Jr.

Calvary Rectory,
61 Gramercy Park North,
New York City.

I

CAUGHT IN MUFTI

IN summer, Calvary Church goes out to the people who do not come to her. Each clear Sunday night the clergy and a robed volunteer choir march out, singing, to a neighbouring square. There we give, from an informal pulpit, simple, direct testimony of what Christ has done for us.

While these services are planned for the men and women on the park benches, all sorts of people turn up in the crowd. We noticed, one night, a man who looked like a young broker. He was well dressed, and his red necktie gave a touch of colour to his grey summer clothes. We learned his story later when we knew him better. From the time he was a child, there permeated his very definite ambitions for intellectual and worldly success, a desire to give his life to what would bring the greatest good to the most people. He thought of music as a possible outlet, but in the mid-Western university where he was studying he decided finally to enter business. His experience in the Navy during the War was a bitter one. The whole militaristic scheme seemed to him out of gear with the deepest things he knew. It was at this time that a bishop suggested to him the possibility of entering the ministry. He finished his education, which had been interrupted by the War, and graduated from a great mid-Western university at twenty-one, but after a short time in a

packing firm in Chicago he decided to do some gradu-
ate work in the East. From there he went to a Standard Oil Corporation, but more and more he rebelled at
the thought of spending his life in commercial work.
He thought again of the Church. He writes of himself:

"Almost immediately I began to feel that I was
hardly suited to enter a theological seminary. I knew
nothing of such institutions, and I was inclined at that
time to look upon them as havens of sanctity. I knew
that I was not a saint, and as a result I experienced a
feeling of inferiority along with many other fears that
I would not be able to measure up to standards. I
knew all too well that there were certain defeats in my
life, but I had courage enough to believe that I would
find in the seminary a power that would make me
victorious.

"I was agreeably surprised when I entered the
seminary in a large city to find many fine, congenial
men, as well as a number of ' good fellows.' At first
I was happy, but, later on in my first year, I found
that I had not experienced or learned to live a quality
of life that gave me victory over self. Much to my
chagrin, I found myself joining with the ' good fellows.'
During my second year I led a life that was little short
of debauchery. All of the time I kept up my studies
to a very high standard. In the meantime I became
more and more defeated until I plainly realized that I
could not get away from self even in sin. In my last
year I sought other means of helping me forget. My
spare time was given over to theatres, the opera, con-
certs, and mingling with friends in the city. Fine as
these things were, they did not solve my problems, nor
meet my longings.

"At the close of school I sailed for Europe. There

I had a complete rest and picked up sufficient courage to return to my diocese in the Middle West to assume charge of a church. As clergy were very scarce, and since I was young and of good background, my bishop sent me to a town of twenty thousand, with two colleges. I found the people were rather conservative and somewhat content with what seemed to me an impossible situation. The church building was almost sixty years old, really quite unsafe, and altogether inadequate for present day needs. Immediately I found what little enthusiasm I had stored up, slipping away, and by Christmas I was miserably unhappy.

"A new church must come first, so I thought, and thus four months after my arrival I started (without even a thought or a prayer as to whether God wanted it) to campaign for a new building. Money was scarce, people were hard to inspire, and all in all it was a heavy up-hill pull. By this time I had almost ceased to pray, for I could not see that it did any good. But being equipped with a great physique, I managed to pull the thing through in my own strength, and the dedication took place on a day in June, 1928, much to the joy of everyone but myself. All the praise and congratulations only made me feel worse. I had led a congregation in the building of the most beautiful church in town, but I could not get away from the fact that I had failed miserably in my two years in the ministry. I knew what ministers are supposed to do, and I had not done that. I had not changed a single life. I had failed people in trouble and in the hour of need. There was no getting away from that.

" When all the fuss of dedication had died down, I was anxious to get away. Maybe I could forget. I accepted an invitation to preach in one of the largest and wealthiest churches in New York City during the month of August, while I was on vacation. On my way east I stopped in Chicago to visit some seminary friends, and on one occasion had dinner with one of them who had been in charge of a parish similar to my own. I learned that he had been going through some of the things that had made me so unhappy, but, strange to say, he had found a way out. He had been, so he told me, to a School of Life in Calvary Parish, New York City. I knew Calvary Parish, and the year before I had read with much interest Mr. Shoemaker's book, *Children of the Second Birth*. I had been impressed then with the fact that 'those people' had something that I did not have. However, I had no idea how to get it. When I heard my friend talking about the work at Calvary, and when I saw what it had done for him, I was more determined than ever to view the work for myself.

" On my arrival in New York I learned that services were being held in Madison Square on each Sunday evening by a group of people from Calvary Parish. I arrived on the spot, which was very well known to me, a bit before seven. When I saw the vested choir and clergy marching in procession, preceded by a crucifer bearing a large wooden cross, and the entire group lustily singing ' Onward, Christian Soldiers,' my good Episcopal spine quivered, for I had never, even in my rashest moments, expected to see this come to pass. A crowd of one hundred and fifty gathered about the soap-box pulpit. I, dressed in my most unclerical outfit, was standing hard by, trying to appear very nonchalant, but yet at the same time inwardly straining every fibre to hear what was said. I was convicted on the spot by the reality that these people possessed.

Never before had street preachers touched me like that, because in my estimation they had covered up their experience with too much emotion and too many amens. But here were people like myself, getting up on a box, and telling in a very humble way what Christ had done for them. What was more, I plainly saw that He had done something for them. More painful still, I realized that they were doing something that I could not do, and furthermore, they had had an experience that had never come to me. Here was what I had hoped to find in the seminary, and I was determined to get it.

"At the regular services later on at Calvary, I met the rector, and he invited me to have lunch with him. I was glad of this opportunity, for I felt I might get some new ideas which would be of service to me in my parish back home. During the lunch and afterwards we discussed the work at Calvary, and then my parish in the West, finally getting around to *myself*. No one, high or low, had ever talked to me as he did, and yet I liked it, because I knew for the first time in my life I had met a man who really understood me and wanted to show me the way out; he sensed my need and was frank enough to tell me of it. He finally got me to the point of realizing that to change people you must be changed yourself. I could not get away from that. I knew that was absolute truth. I left him that day with a sense of release that I had never experienced before. Somehow I felt better, and yet I knew I had not gone the full way. I started going to Thursday night group meetings, and having lunch with various members of the group, and every contact seemed to convict me more and more.

" Finally, on the evening of August 23, I attended

a Thursday night group meeting, and it was there that I heard two clergymen speak, one of whom was a bishop. What these two men said rendered the knock-out blow to my pride, and after the meeting I walked home with the rector, determined to make a surrender of my life. This conversion business puzzled me. I did not know how to go about it, and I was too timid to ask. I could not conceive of anything happening to me such as happened to St. Paul in apostolic times. But in our conversation we got down to ' brass tacks,' and before long I had brought out into the open a number of what we old-fashionedly call *sins*, which were blocking me from communion with God. Right then and there I surrendered those specific sins and all the others which I might discover later but which I could not recall or recognize then as sins. Both of us got down on our knees, he praying for me first, and then I prayed for God's forgiveness and without any reservations I handed my life over to God for Him to use as He saw fit—not as I saw fit. There was no white light, and not a great deal of emotion, but immediately there came a feeling of peace and release. But I know all too well that I cannot ride on the glory of that first surrender for the remainder of my life. It is not a question of being converted once and for all time, but rather it is a question of successively giving up new areas as the realization comes that you have been ' holding out on God.' It is by this means that Guidance becomes more and more real and that one feels more and more the Power of God's Holy Spirit taking possession."

While in charge of the church in up-town Manhattan, he had come to know one of the staff, and with her he often talked concerning the experiences which were coming to him. He found her a sympathetic listener, somewhat prejudiced by what she had heard about our work. Then he found that she, too, whom he considered something of a saint, had also her own unhappy problems in her life and work. Witty, human, gifted she must have been always, but many a church-worker has never given these gifts to God: her church-work is in one compartment, her touch with the world in another. She began to come down with him. Instead of what she had heard, she found a crowd of very happy people, obviously possessed of more power and joy than she was finding in her religion. Soon after he had made his decision to surrender to Christ, she made a further surrender; and the general aspiration of many years became a personal commitment, the vague desire to serve became a message for individuals. Soon she reached another member of the staff with whom she worked, bringing this girl to a decision for Christ which was deeper and more far-reaching than she had ever made. I shall not forget hearing her tell of her work in an annual church conference where, the year before, she had not helped one life, but where this year about a dozen girls were brought to decision through the work which she, and two girls in the " group," were able to do.

In the autumn Caught in Mufti went back to his parish again, stopping off for a week's house-party on the way, where the experience was solidified and where he met many more members of the Fellowship. " The first thing I did when I got home," he writes, " was to tell my people exactly what had happened to me while I was away. I can say with all honesty that no single action in my ministry ever did more to win the hearts and confidences of those people than that simple talk about the change which had come into my life. Immediately I set out, not over-zealously but guidedly, to help others find what I had found. I made mistakes; I even failed; but God did not fail me. I found it hard going at times, but there was one thing which was inescapable, and that was the peace and joy of the experience which had begun in the summer. I never doubted the reality of that experience of Christ."

During the winter some of us from Calvary were privileged to go to his parish for a week's mission. "At that time," he writes, " there were a number of changes made in the lives of our people. The first person changed was the organist. She is a young woman of the finest Christian background, who has always been interested in the church, but somehow she had missed the real power and lacked an incentive for what she was doing. Selfishness, pettiness and temper had made life difficult for herself and for others. Now she saw how definite sin was blocking her from Christ. Early in the mission she made a real decision for Him, and registered it at one of the evening meetings. Her honesty broke down the reserve of her best friend, also one of our faithful workers. She came, saying she wanted the same thing. All her life she had put her best energy into the church, but she often got into trouble and had her feelings hurt, because she lacked love and sensitiveness towards those with whom she worked. Her surrender has made her a much more loving and a much more effective person.

"Another woman in the parish had been an agnostic and had gone through a struggle for her faith. She came to church seeking some consolation and assurance. I talked with her many hours about the Christ of experience, and she listened with interest but could not seem to bring herself to decision. One day she came to tell me of the need in the life of one of her close friends. For the first time she did some really deep sharing, concerning a problem which happened to parallel the problem of her friend in trouble. This seemed a direct challenge from God to use her experience for the benefit of the other person. She accepted the challenge, and it marked the beginning of a long and guided series of events in those two lives. With absolute trust in God, with much prayer and love, her friend was brought through a miserably unhappy domestic situation to the solution of her problems, a provision for herself and her children, and a real and glowing experience of Christ.

"As a result of these and other decisions for Christ, a small group of committed people was begun for the purpose of deepening their experience and of training leadership. A young matron, very much engrossed in social life but miserably unhappy, found real joy and radiance through the work of the group. Another young married woman, full of self-pity, highly nervous and full of worries, found something real in the church for the first time in her life. It is not always easy to give the results of such a spiritual adventure. But, as rector of the parish, I could see a change in the attitude of many people. There were no serious cliques, but there had been precious little co-operation and almost no Christian fellowship: the leaven of the mission had far-reaching effects in every nook and corner of the parish.

" Two college lads strayed into my house one night

after service. I found them agnostics who hoped there might yet be something in Christianity. Both had thought of studying for the ministry, but God was now a big question mark, and they could by no means think of Him as personal. At first I met them upon this purely intellectual level of their own choosing, but I saw that we were not getting very far. To them religion was something to be carried round in one's head: it had not actually touched their lives. After a good many talks, one of these boys found that Christ could still change lives. With no persuasion on my part, he sought confirmation, and became the first candidate for the ministry this parish had had in sixty years of its existence, and this in a city where there are two colleges.

" But, after all, the greatest miracle seems to be myself and the difference which this experience of Christ has made in my life-work. Every phase of the work became more easy and natural. If I can take the word of friends, it made a difference in the appeal of what I said in my pulpit. I soon began to discover in living on guidance that God does have a plan for us and that it is very different from living on a hap-hazard basis, as it appeared to me at first. There went the sense of stress and worry. Previously I had gone out seeking contacts with people, but now I found them coming to me, both from inside and outside the church. In looking over my records for a period of three months, I find that I have had one hundred and twenty-five interviews about Christ and personal religion, some of which lasted as long as six or seven hours.

"A certain man who was healed by our Lord was asked by his friends how it came about. In reply he could only say, ' Whereas I was blind, now I see.'   In a similar way this much do I know, that whereas I was discouraged, defeated and powerless, on the verge of leaving the ministry altogether, I now feel happy, victorious and powerful, and would not trade my job for any other in the world."

II

OBLITERATING THE DEAD-LINE

MOST of the stories in this book concern relatively young men. But the message here set forth would be very inadequate indeed if it had nothing to say to the man with much of his ministry behind him, with a set to his life which makes change more difficult. Hugh Black says that as a man grows older he hears the sound of closing doors about him. One of those doors lets upon true spiritual effectiveness when life is in its afternoon, and the temptation is great never to try that door again: to accept one's spiritual defeats as one accepts one's grey hair, with good grace but with finality. It is the way of young-mindedness to treat one's spiritual defects as a problem, not a fate: and it is the happy province of faith in God to keep men young in their minds, ready to meet a new call, willing to " go up higher " towards a better level of life and service.

The man of whom this article is written is slightly above the half-century mark. He is physically vigorous and mentally conversant with the latest thought-life of the day. The new books are in his library, and he is not tongue-tied when modern ideas come up for discussion. He occupies a pulpit of fair importance in his church, and is often in demand for special occasions. In no sense of the word would he be called a " problem " in the ministry. He has travelled widely, and was entrusted with one very important post-war service by his denomination. Europe and its affairs are as familiar to him as his own historic state in New England. He tells me that his real heart is in the mission field, which he prefers to a satiated America. But because of failing budgets the work which was to have been his life-work was discontinued, and he finds himself back in America trying to contribute his part in reviving a great denomination which, he says, " once led the world in evangelism, and now lags behind, trying almost in vain to whip up a flagging interest in the winning of the world." His own colleagues and the leaders of his church express themselves as gratified by the contribution which he is making.

In middle life, this well-trained preacher, a " Doctor " not by courtesy but by dint of earning it in one of our great universities, found himself crowded down into cramped quarters, and evidently destined to small things. His missionary experience counted for little in a church where at best missionary interest was on the decline. His war experience, and his work in a prominent field of service, unfitted him for a time to minister to small crowds and deal with petty financial problems. It wants some grace for a man who has preached to thousands to begin preaching to a trifle over a hundred. Where he had handled budgets of thirty and forty thousand dollars, and more than once been called on to administer much larger sums, he found himself confronted by close, hard-headed, unimaginative business men who pinched the pennies and allowed him a closely-watched oversight of paltry budgets of a few thousands. He could not adapt himself to these confining restrictions. He longed for larger fields, to call out all his powers and offer some respectable resistance to his abilities; and this could hardly be concealed always from his people, who must have dimly realized that his heart was elsewhere. Restlessness seized him, and kept him always looking towards the green of distant fields. For three years he tormented himself by seeking a way out. Sorrow came. He had known sorrow before. Day and night memory haunted him. Life readjusted itself gradually to the repeated blows. A woman of spiritual character and charming ways made him forget the old heartaches which had made of life a thing of constant pain and scarcely to be desired. Their home became a haven of delight to " weary ones in needful hour " because of the love and happiness of it.

At last a call came—back to former fields, back to the regions of his early ministry where he had, years ago, achieved measurable spiritual success. It was a call, he says, which " placed my feet again on the rungs of a ladder which I might climb. My friends rejoiced in my return and predicted a speedy advancement." He calls the church " a middle-class church," and says that he " uses the adjective in a complimentary sense, and considers himself to belong to that same class." He is of Puritan ancestry, and he was born of a long line of good stock: but he is the first clergyman in over three centuries of the family history, and perhaps the first college-trained man which appears in the records. His parents were unpretentious people. His mother was deeply devout and inclined to mysticism. She longed to see her husband and three sons " in the Kingdom," and her wish for the youngest, who is the subject of this sketch, was that he might be a preacher of the Gospel.

He tells me that while he was in second year of High School a religious experience of the old sort shook him emotionally to the depths, but remained with him for good in the choice of religion as the chief interest of his life, and of the ministry as his work. He was thought by all his friends to be assured of large usefulness in the major emphasis of his denomination, evangelism. He took to it eagerly. He won many lives for Christ, and was often sought after by men less gifted in evangelism to make the personal appeal for surrender to Christ.

"Then," he says, "the evangelistic note grew weaker. Critical study, foreign travel, the 'social gospel' and religious education claimed my attention. My interest in making the social order truly Christian is at present the chief concern also of my denomination. The leaders of my church are the moral backbone to many social reforms. But the conviction began to deepen in me that these movements were lacking the motive power which might make them effective. I saw the church losing members. I saw my beloved missionary work languish for want of funds. That, too, in America, rich beyond the dreams of the ages! Something seemed to be the matter. Somewhere men were missing the way to the City of God. Church people cared more for their radio and their automobiles than they did for their church, perhaps more than for their Christ. They did not seem to care: and I was one preacher who cared that they did not care. I was hungry for the manifestation of the power of religion to change lives. I felt myself to be a failure in the very work which had once been my joy and delight."

This sense of failure was reflected in his preaching.

The old note of triumph was drowned out in a censoriousness which he called the note of prophecy, but which was in fact plain fault-finding begotten of his own disappointment. In this he was fortified also by much of the so-called progressive preaching of the day, which tends often towards cynicism. To be critical, even cynical, of one's day and generation is not difficult: but to be truly prophetic and constructive is another matter. Denunciatory preaching is apt to become personal: he found it easy to slam leaders. " I believed my heart intended only good, but it was not unpleasant to watch the arrows of sarcasm as they left the pulpit. I knew the weak places in my people's armour, and I felt called upon to run the lance in just there. I did not want to be harsh or mean, but the notes I sounded were censorious and sometimes bitter."

There came a day when this took its toll. He found himself " the most unpopular preacher " he had ever met. The crowd dwindled away and left him. A disgruntled membership were the echoes of his own voice. Fault-finding is contagious, and his church came to be known as a breeder of it. In less than a year, matters had moved so far that he felt there was no retrieving them, and he had better move elsewhere.

Then a friend accidentally left at his house a copy of a modern book of changed lives.* " I took but a few hours to read it through," he says, " and came to the conclusion that here was the note I had been leaving out of my ministry, the note of personal responsibility for those without spiritual experience or

---

* *Children of the Second Birth*, by S. M. Shoemaker, Jr., Fleming H. Revell Company.

interest. Shortly after came a meeting with Frank
Buchman, and the testimonies of changed lives at a
glorious house-party near by. This particular group
seemed to be composed mostly of the comfortably
well-to-do, but superficial distinctions were soon lost
in the evident sincerity and willingness to confess to
sin and failure. I knew I had landed in the right
crowd. They made a deep impression upon me. The
Quiet Hours and the sharing of experiences were
begun at home, and vitalized family devotions, so
that the entire family saw the result in a new spirit.
I found my own spiritual life going forward by rapid,
natural strides. And for the first time in years I knew
a sense of the victorious in my own life. This was
followed by victory in the church, increasing victory
which continues. I seemed unable to keep off the
streets making calls, even during the morning, so
fascinating did pastoral work suddenly become. Our
mid-week meeting received a fresh access of power.
New witnesses appeared, with fresh testimony to
recent experiences. The prayer-meeting actually became a factor in the church-life again. A true source
of power had been tapped. People frequently asked
for prayers. New faces were seen. Even front pews
were filled. The prayer-service had to be followed
by an auxiliary hour at the parsonage. To my aston-
ishment, this second meeting grew till the rooms were
often over-crowded by eager people who forgot time,
and found it quite possible to stay an hour after mid-
week meeting and then to come again to a special
' Fellowship Group ' which took up another week-day
evening. Instead of one poorly attended, listless
prayer-service, there are now two groups meeting
regularly, and the heat of summer seems to have had

no diminishing effect. I have given up my vacation for the sake of people who need constant nurture, and I am having the best kind of a vacation, of change if not of rest, in watching my church revive." At this writing it is mid-summer, but his prayer-meetings are larger than ever and steadily growing. He says, "A new spirit of power is everywhere present and apparent. People are steadily finding God."

One morning in staff at Calvary the " Fool for Christ " * said that she had had guidance to go to the city where this man's church is situated, and work there for several days. During the period of her stay, the pastor tells me, influenza was raging, and there were three cases in his own house, where she stayed. A few personal conferences were arranged, but the people were afraid both of influenza and of the possibility of some new form of fanaticism. But he says, " the worker from Calvary was most human, and indeed thrilling in her cheerful approach to people."

One of the church-leaders found a real experience, and this was the gist of her testimony: " You all know me. I have been in the church for years. I have been President of the Ladies' Aid and a teacher in the Church School and in almost every form of church-activity. You all know what I have been in church work. Now, I want to tell you that I have made my surrender to Christ and I am very happy." This was a woman who had not come to prayer-meeting for years, felt that being busied with church-fairs and suppers was enough, had been full of fault-finding, and did not at all like her pastor's

* *Children of the Second Birth.*

emphasis on personal evangelism. Now she became his ally and began to plan for the capturing of other leaders for the Fellowship. Her first testimony brought a look of amazement into the faces of the company. But that testimony was repeated in growing power through the weeks following, as she grew in the new experience which had come.

In a tea-room, the minister and his wife had gotten interested in one of the waitresses: she was vivacious and had agreeable manners, but they noted that she always liked to talk with strangers about her evidently unsatisfied life. It was found that she had once been a member of their denomination: but disappointment in her home life, where strain had reached near the breaking-point, had driven her to uncertain company where gin was the source of cordiality. For her the future looked hardly worth the living. She wondered at the evident happiness of this minister and his wife. She craved it in her own home, where six little ones had to listen to constant wrangling and feel the pinch of poverty. Then came sickness, and the need for a serious operation. The minister's wife felt led to stop in and ask for her, and heard that she was at the hospital. She and her husband went together, and found the waitress almost despairing. Life held too little for her to want to live much longer—but here stood the minister and his wife, whom she had wanted to see, but been too proud to call for in time of trouble. They stayed with her till she found peace, which resulted in a quiet all-night sleep before her operation. The pastor wakened her a few moments before the ether-cone blotted out all consciousness, and they had prayer together; the waitress prayed, " Oh God, help me to come back a

Christian girl, or not to come back." In her own
longing to find God, or else to stop living, even the
children were forgotten. She came back—back to
life and health and home. After a few weeks of
suffering and convalescence, she came to one of the
meetings, alone. Her testimony brought tears to the
eyes of many. The pastor could hardly believe it
was the same girl. Culture and refinement showed in
every word, the culture of a true heart, educated in
the Spirit. Next Sunday she brought her husband.
When the invitation was given his hand shot up. He
found God that day. Then service after service,
week after week, she came, bringing one or two new
people. Friends and relatives came with her. She
was the radiant centre of new life. A noticeable little
crowd gathered about her at the meetings. The little
waitress became a true evangelist, going from friend
to friend with a transforming message. After four
months, the minister was interested to count how
many people had begun coming regularly to the
weekly meetings at her instigation; and there were
twenty of them. She goes on with her waiting, and
there are problems still: but her life is remade.

" So it has gone with me," he writes. " I am not
surrounded by crowds: my church is still small and,
like myself, middle-class. But I must say that it is becoming a marked centre of spiritual life. (This was
verified for me recently by the testimony of one of his
fellow-ministers in his town.) Where once I seemed to
have reached the limit of my power and usefulness, it
is now evident that I can continue to look forward to
increasing service. My entire ministry has undergone
a profound change. My sermons are no longer carefully treated *themes:* the preparation is still thorough,

but the *subjects* have changed.   Now the sermons grow out of clinical observation.   People say to me that the old note of harshness and censoriousness is gone, and they hear a voice of pleading and they realize the love of God through what is said.   No longer is there tedium in ringing door-bells: the pastor in me has been reborn.   People come for help.   Young people especially.   Sundays bring groups of people about my wife and myself in church and at our house.   There is evident expectancy on all sides.   Life in the church has been reborn.   And for me the dead-line has been obliterated."

III

LIVING IN THE LIGHT

ONE of the most frequent attendants at house-parties and other gatherings of the First Century Christian Fellowship is a young man of twenty-six, with a bright eye, a strong jaw, a sincerity which would be oppressive if he did not break into laughter now and then, and a good mind with considerable literary talent.

He comes of missionary parentage, and his father is one of the most widely useful and beloved men whom it has ever been my privilege to know. The home in which this son was born is one of beauty and harmony, a place where one feels the Master as a constant Guest. And so, he says, " My childhood religion was a natural and happy affair. A missionary's life is of the frontier variety, and things spiritual must be a reality to him, or he will go under, for he touches paganism in a manner unknown to most ministers at home. In the field the Church and the world are not at peace, but at war, as they were meant to be. Good is never so attractive as when it is in conflict with evil. The spiritual life of our family included the servants, and I remember one of them as a young catechumen who had been in prison for his faith; and how our nurse was won through the devoted love of my mother. Facts like these were part of my own early experience, bringing conviction

46

of the reality of God, the power of Christ, and the practical nature of prayer.

"At eight there came a change for me. It is one of the tragedies of a missionary's life that he must send his children away from home very early if they are to be properly educated. I went to a British school founded primarily for children of that marvellous witness to the guiding and providing power of God, the China Inland Mission, whose workers live not by salary but by faith and prayer, and have penetrated the farthest recesses of all China's provinces. The spiritual atmosphere was warm and realistic. Everyone believed that the world was created in 4004 B. C. But the plain fare and the Sundays of Eton collars and Bible reading and the restrictions about seeing anything of the girls in their near-by school provided a mental and spiritual discipline for which I have always been grateful.

"After four years' work at our own schools in China, I came to America. I was sent to one of the best schools, as I think, in the country, where the Headmaster is a consecrated man. When my first moral problem arose, I went to him with it. He was very understanding, gave me absolution and some sound advice, and urged me to see him again. But he was busy, and though I knew he cared tremendously about my spiritual life, I did not seek him out again. His help was temporary. More and more the idea of God and the facts of my moral life grew apart, until I forgot that there was any connection."

At college, friends came easily. By the end of Freshman year, there had come hard-earned recognition in the social and intellectual life of the class. Studies were interesting. Work on the college paper, crew and tennis, and the engaging novelty of club life filled in the rest of the picture. He had some older friends in the ministry who kept before him the possibility of the ministry as a profession. But he was still carrying about a struggle for which he found no help. The religious people he knew were of the Liberal school, and did not believe in the confessional. He grew undisciplined about writing letters, punctuality, strict honesty in accounts. He told nobody anything about himself.

"All this did not keep me from interest in religion," he says. " My room-mate had achieved the rank of atheist, and I rather wished I had the courage to join him. Yet, on the other hand, there were my parents: Christianity must be true! The Church must be worth something for so many of my friends had given their lives to its service. So I defended Christianity and the Church with arguments which made up in stubbornness what they lacked in conviction. Christianity was then for me a matter of opinion, not of experience. I think it never remotely occurred to me that it might be the solution to my own eternal battle.

" In the middle of my Junior year I went to one of the great Student Volunteer Conferences in the Middle West. I told my family, in effect, that I should give Christianity a ' last chance,' and if I found nothing real in it I should throw it over. There were eight thousand delegates, and an impressive list of speakers with topics covering every range of possible approach to the problems of Christianity as a philosophy of life. Our delegation did not seem to believe in prayer as much as most of the others, being very self-consciously intellectual by training.

No one in the whole elaborate process tried to get at my own needs, and the moral cause of my scepticism. I left full of ideas, but lacking what I came to find.

" Getting back to college I found a letter from my father, asking in a rather casual way whether I had ever run across a certain Frank Buchman, who had once been at our home in China. I thought little about it, until a couple of weeks later when a friend of mine invited me to attend a week-end group at a village inn not far from where we lived. Mr. Buchman, he said, would be there. I went, hardly knowing why. About twenty of us gathered at supper on Friday evening. Afterwards I waited for the conventional address of the evening. There was none. Instead, we went round the circle, saying who we were and why we came, and what, if anything, we were looking for. Most, like me, seemed to be looking for something without being able to say what. There was much laughter and naturalness, and no pretense. It was a relief to be oneself, and say what one thought about religion and life. ' Certainly,' I thought, ' it must have taken something out of the ordinary to induce that handsome Scotch giant to throw in his lot with it all, or to create any spiritual enthusiasm in that rake from the Law School.'

" Next day we listened to stories with their settings all over the world. One of them centred round our summer home in China. They concerned ordinary people such as I had known all my life, but something had happened to them. Somehow this remote thing called religion had seeped down into their hearts and wills and muscles. Hitherto I had approached religion from the theoretical angle, seeking to relate this principle to life. Here *was* life. As time went on, I said to myself that this was all bunk, or else it was a real answer. I was in no mood for casuistry. Could there be any men present who could fully understand me and my problems? I heard enough frank admissions of all sorts of moral and spiritual failure to know that these men wore no masks. I argued with a young minister about the value of Confucianism, and the danger of jumping in until one was sure of one's ethical system. But I did not fool him—he knew I was sparring. That evening another man was sensitive enough to my need to tell me personally about his own experience of Christ, and about another man who had been released. Hardly knowing what I did, I told him all about myself. He took what I said sympathetically but almost casually. We talked about how sin can prevent a man from knowing God. I saw for the first time that honesty with others about oneself was the first step in the knowledge of God.

"At a subsequent house-party I began to think about the ministry. So far as I had gone with religious experience, it was giving me a better grasp on life than I had ever had before, and it was natural to begin thinking about giving myself to it full-time. Those I met at the house-parties never so much as mentioned the ministry to me. Their concern was for the kind of life we live in the present. Their assumption was that were God once to become real now, the future would take care of itself. The ministry, they seemed to feel, was a meaningless vocation unless it was the spontaneous expression of a religious experience. To bring about this experience, they began far up-stream. They taught me that the proving-ground of religious sincerity was moral earnestness: only by this should I find God, and know His will for my life. There was something more important even than being a minister. That was to be a Christian.

" Well, it didn't last. And because it didn't there were many, including myself, who were quick to explain how this sort of emotional crisis never *does* last. But as I look back, the facts were these. This was the highest type of life being lived by young men that I had seen. But it was correspondingly demanding. Such emotion as I had been exposed to was what Benjamin Kidd called the ' emotion of the ideal.' The thing which I saw, translated into human society, would make a new world. This was represented by a Fellowship who expected from one another nothing short of the best, held each other to the highest, and made a practice of withholding nothing from one another, time, money, experience, which would help to achieve the ideal. Such living in the light was fatal to compromise. Life without compromise was a large order. It was one thing to want to clean up the areas of one's life which were plainly unpleasant, but to risk one's whole future in the interests of a still rather hazy ideal was quite another thing. Senior year was intensely absorbing intellectually and socially. Since further association with these people who had brought me spiritually thus far, meant yielding realms where I felt I could stand alone, I cut their acquaintance. It was pretty crude gratitude after they had given of themselves to me, and to blur that fact, I criticized. I said nothing scandalous: I just cast gentle and supercilious ridicule on guidance, sudden conversion, and sharing.

"After college I spent a very interesting year teach-

ing in China. There were several experiences which
I remember. One was an encounter with a Funda-
mentalist friend of mine whose Fundamentalism was
his whole message. He hammered his theology at
me, but nothing happened. He said I wasn't converted, and I said conversion might be all right for
some people, but not for all—there were 'many roads,'
and ventilated all the stock ideas I have so often
listened to from other people. He never mentioned
the moral claims of Christ, or what He could do for
people's moral needs. He just conducted one end of
an intellectual sparring match. I saw the futility of
such an approach. I was trying to teach history and
literature to my Chinese boys, and now and then a
little religion. But I made small progress spiritually.
I found it not so hard to make them like me, and
they came round to my study one evening a week.
But those groups never went very deep. I did not
dare to go deep, because I knew I had not wholly
faced my own needs, and I might have to take too
much of my own medicine. The boys must have
sensed my lack of forthrightness in it all, for the
groups were 'sticky.' I do not think the year was
wasted, but I found out that personal indecision was
enough to undercut such moral influence as I tried
to radiate.

"Another experience of great interest to me was the
result of my increasing interest in political affairs.
The year 1925-6 will probably go down in history as
the birth-year of modern China. Travelling overland,
with a commission from an American journal for a
series of articles, I came to Canton, the revolutionary
centre of the country. There I met Michael Borodin,
chief Soviet advisor to the Nationalist government.

In him I saw one of the few men I had met who were really translating their convictions into life. He held convictions with which instinctively I disagreed: ' You,' he said, ' are trying to bring in the new world by love. We are trying to bring it by force—that is the difference.' But on another occasion, striding up and down his office, he shot out between cigar-puffs the impatient reminder: ' You Christians have a religion you are willing to die for. I want to tell you that I have a religion also which I am willing to die for.' There was no doubt that he had. But with regard to my own religion, it struck me that here was one more man who took me for granted. I knew that I should not be willing to die for Chris-tianity. I realized with a start that I held no con-victions about it which were worth dying for.

" But for all my uncertainties, I felt that the Church was the best available agency for being of use in the world. So I went to the seminary. At the end of my first year, I realized acutely that some-thing must be done. Sometimes during that year, when pressed by my agnostic friends for proofs of religion, I would point to men in the Fellowship whose lives had been changed. In a world whose greatest stricture against the Church was its want of vitality, these lives were impressive facts. I knew that that sort of vitality was lacking in me. I was learning much in my theology courses, but it was not along these lines; the assumption was that a man must already have had a real experience of Christ before he should decide for the ministry, so that it was not the function of the seminary to convert its students.

" They have in England an expression ' all out,'

connoting what we might call one hundred per cent allegiance. This fits the need I felt at this time to find something large enough to command my uncompromising loyalty. There were occasional inspired moments when I sensed in a flash the possibilities of my life if wholly given to Christ. But the way seemed too studded with forbidding negatives. I must be 'all out' for the Christian religion, or else 'all out' against it. The whole thing partook of the quality which I felt in the Fellowship: Christianity was bunk, or else it was an answer.

" It was in this mood that I went to another house-party. I resented what seemed the group's demand for agreement. I expected to receive a good deal of unpleasant attention. I was left politely alone to chew my own cud. It hurt my pride, but it produced in me the most serious thinking I had ever done. It was the radiant life of these people that held me. There was an undercurrent, beneath all the merriment, of earnestness, an edge of iron which distinguished this from much of the intellectualized and humanized religion I had seen. Again one felt the swing and gayety of it was irresistible.

"At these affairs one has a chance to get perspective on the past and the future. I had wanted for a long time to help people on the deepest levels, yet person after person I had failed—men in China, in Russia, at home. The house-parties showed me men who had the secret which I lacked. They had paid the price for it. Five fears held me fast: fear of losing place, centering in the ambition to write, not for the glory of God except incidentally, but for personal advancement; fear for reputation, for while this Fellowship was growing in power, it was still widely discredited, slandered and ostracised, and identification with it would mean a certain amount of contempt from men I admired; fear of losing my intellectual integrity, were I to submit my will to God, and live on a basis of God's guidance; fear of losing my sense of humour if I should go in for anything so absorbing; and fear of losing my friends if I should take too decided a stand about religion. I reached my decision slowly. A young Scotch doctor and I thrashed out the issues one evening and arrived at this result quite logically: we believed in a God who cared for us. Then we must hold that His will for us must be the best possible investment for our lives, and the finding of it our chief concern. If what He demanded seemed to involve the yielding of anything that we held dear, plainly one of two results would follow: either He would give us back the plan which we had surrendered, with His sanction, or else He would give us something better in its place. The shift in point of view came over a period of days. My chief feeling at the time, I remember, was that whatever it might bring, it was growingly inevitable, and that being the case I had better see it through as quickly as possible. I remember sitting on the outskirts of a large group one evening, and saying that if this happy, out-and-out thing were Christianity, I was for it.

" This experience, which I consider was my conversion, brought to me a kind of life which was entirely new to me. The fears were proved foolish. There was an integration of scattered impulses. I had victory where I never expected to have it. The daily Quiet Times helped tremendously in concentration and the ordering of each day. I was given the power, through sharing to the limit of my own experience, of helping others in a way which had been impossible on the old basis of human companionship only. Theology became vital, and preparation for the ministry a romance of discovery and expectation. The Church and the Bible had a new meaning. Such sayings as, 'Ye must be born again,' and 'He that loseth his life for my sake . . . shall find it,' and 'Seek ye first the kingdom . . . and all these things shall be added,' became living to me as part of my own experience. Previously I had gone just far enough into Christianity to feel the burden of the law, and not far enough to reap the joy of the Spirit. Now things were different.

"The fruits have been all too meagre in others' lives. The pride of spiritual achievement has been a problem for some time. I am learning slowly and painfully that God can only fully work through a selfless soul. My pride and undue criticism of others in the Church have sometimes hindered more effective work. But there have been some who have been really helped.

"One was a youngster of twenty who works in a factory, and does job-printing on the side. I had been asked to preach in the church where he was much interested in the Young People's Society. The sermon was personal, and after the service I saw him standing round, looking 'hungry,' and as if he wanted to talk. We slipped into a pew and began to talk. He ventilated his objections to some of the Old Testament stories and New Testament miracles. I said nothing. Then he talked about evolution. I still said nothing. Finally he looked up and said, 'Well, I've beaten all round the bush, haven't I? Now I suppose I had better tell you what the trouble is.' I shared with him some of my own needs, and we got down to the thing that was most on his mind. It was pretty elemental. He had never been able to be frank with his parents or anybody else about what was bothering him most. He told the young people of the change in his life. Last time I saw him he was going to get into touch with one of his factory friends, and tell about his experience."

Links are picked up and carried on in interesting and strange ways in a Fellowship like this. If the reader should happen to read a previous book of mine, *Children of the Second Birth,* he will find a reference on pages 31 and 32 to a man who for more than three years called himself a " barren field." Several people had been occasionally in touch with him, but nothing seemed to happen. In a wedding-party he and the subject of this story met. The " barren field " sketched his previous contact with the Fellowship with an odd mixture of nonchalance, bravado and real wistfulness. The two men reached the reception together and went down the receiving line, and while waiting for the guests to file through they talked some more, as they had done the night before. He felt free by now to say what was in his heart, and he said frankly that he was at the end of his rope, and perhaps we were right, after all. There was not much time, and they needed to make the best of it. There was plainly some great problem worrying him, the confession of which would be extremely difficult. He doubted if there were any way out. ' What was the use of talking? ' But still he wanted to talk. He was told that he would need to make a clean breast of it with someone before he would have any peace. He looked at the other man for several seconds. It was a leap, but something had to be done.

"I thought I knew what it was, and asked him point blank. He nodded an assent, but would say no more; went out of the room slamming the door."

They got upstairs just in time for the bridal picture. At the dinner, he sat next to the Militant Mystic, who told him of a house-party beginning in a few days, and invited him to go. This intrigued him and he said he would go. Talking together, the Militant Mystic gave him a vivid picture of what living on faith in total commitment to God and a human fellowship in Christ could mean. He stayed in town for the night, and the next morning had weakened in his decision to go to the house-party, said that he had friends coming for the week-end and he couldn't come. The Militant Mystic, as he left, simply held out his hand and said:

"You do as you are led, but just remember that nothing ever stands in the way of the Lord."

The subject of this sketch got to the house-party on Friday. On Saturday came a special delivery from the "barren field," saying that his friends had come, and stayed only three hours: he expressed deep gratitude for their talks, and asked for a luncheon date. Then he was called on the long distance telephone, and asked to come down for the evening meeting (he was a couple of hours' train journey away), and he said he would, and took the next train, arriving in the middle of the meeting. They had a long talk that night, during which more of the story came out, and they prayed together. Next day he was most uncomfortable, and felt miserable through an afternoon service at which he played the hymns. They ate

supper together that night, and he scarcely touched a
mouthful. Then they went out on the terrace and
sat down. He said it was a question of whether he
would face the whole problem of restoration, especially of telling his parents certain things about himself which they deserved to know. Doubts and fears
tormented him. Time after time he turned almost in
anger, saying it was no use, time was wasted over
him, he simply could not make the decision. There
was nothing to do but pray, and the other man says
that he never felt so vividly the sense of a colossal
battle going on in a man's soul between the hosts of
evil and the armies of light. It was a real valley of
decision. Finally they went into the evening group
which was just about to begin. The Militant Mystic
was about to open the meeting, but walked out with
them instead, and the " barren field " told him briefly
the story. They all prayed together and gave thanks
for his courage and honesty. He had decided by this
time to write his parents, and that was the crucial
issue round which his surrender centred. It was the
specific element which tested and proved the validity
of his commitment to God.

That night he wrote his family. The words fairly
flowed. Next morning in his Quiet Time came the
thought that he might go with his new friend to
Europe for further training in stabilizing his own life
and helping others as he had been helped. It seemed
humanly impossible and they did not bother to check
it with others concerned. The practical unbelief involved in this was made clear when another man later
shared the same guidance, that the " barren field "
should go to Europe. It was a tremendous issue for
a man less than a day old spiritually to launch out on

faith, for there was no financial support visible, and it meant difficult adjustments in his business position. He began to doubt how his family would receive the letter, wondered how they would feel about his leaving home, etc., and for a moment the old battle was on again.   But God won, and the next morning, further convinced that the strengthening of his spiritual life was the most important thing in the world for him, and that going to Europe was the obvious way to put that first, he went off to get his passport, and to see the family.   They were with him to the hilt, and understood everything.   This proved to him that God's hand was at work in it all.   Money came from unexpected sources.   His brother, keenly interested, lunched with them the day they sailed.   The whole family came for the farewell at Calvary House before the boat sailed, and sped him off on his first spiritual pilgrimage.   There are terrible struggles with self during such a time as he spent abroad.   The old life came edging and insinuating its way back into his consciousness.   He was lonely sometimes without the old, comfortable associates instead of these strenuous companions, and there was often a sense of floating in thin air without his accustomed securities.   But there was discipline, too, and growth and truer grasp on himself.   He has come through victoriously, and is back at home and at work, more stable, more unified, more useful, more happy than he ever expected that he could be.

May I point out the sheer spiritual hygiene of what our friend calls " living in the light "?   Through the earlier years he lived in the darkness of need and conscious isolation: any psychologist knows what suffering and danger this may mean in adolescence, and how

great is the relief of opening one's heart to someone
who can be trusted. Then he met a group that is
frank about spiritual matters, honest about their sins,
honest about their victories, too, who showed him,
through mutual exchange, a better way, and put that
way where he could get at it.

Gamaliel Bradford, that profound interpreter of the
human heart, says,* " To confide one's troubles, griefs,
and sufferings, to confide one's triumphs and hopes, to
confide one's life experience of all sorts, this is an un-
quenchable, an irresistible longing, from which no one
is altogether free, and which, when it is repressed in
them, is sure to manifest itself in another form." One
needs hardly to say that this may turn into a morbid,
introspective business when it is indulged in for private comfort and satisfaction. But when the object
of thus " living in the light " is the completer understanding and the full redemption of another life, when
the whole purpose and object is towards another and
not towards self, there is probably no healthier or
happier work in the world: it does for the inner mind
and life what exercise and a bath does for the body,
and it relieves, inspires and unspeakably ennobles
other lives. The conspiracy of silence, about sin,
about deliverance, about spiritual experience, has
lasted long enough. This generation is frank about
other things, and they want the truth about what God
does for us.

---

* *Life and I,* Gamaliel Bradford, p. 255.

IV

THE COLLEGE CHAPLAIN

STANDING up some inches beyond six feet, in his Oxford blazer, and usually chuckling good-naturedly, he is an impressively unclerical-looking figure. I have travelled with him for months at a time, and I have yet to see in him a sign of bad temper or the loss of extraordinary poise. Some men's good dispositions appear to be the purely physical effect of healthy glands, and this man is a magnificently healthy specimen: but I have always felt that for him good temper and a serene spirit were a real achievement which have always taken, and still take, effort. His kindliness is radiant. His enthusiasm is as far as possible from fanaticism. He is the kind of a Christian who makes the sceptics wonder whether they have missed something.

He comes of a religious Church of England family. His father is a well-to-do business man, supports good causes, and loves to travel. For his son he incarnated the desirability of security, prosperity and the joy of being able to give. A very gentle mother, with a deep love for the Church, prayed much for him, and without suggesting it too definitely has always wished him to go into the ministry. His family have always been able and glad to give him the best of everything.

He had the usual public school career in England,

most of it spent while the war was still in progress, and conditions were abnormal. The depression of the later years of the war threw its shadow across school life, and made some boys wonder about the meaning of their existence. He tried to think through what he ought to do with himself in this kind of a world, but found no solution to his problem. So he drifted into business when he left school at eighteen, thinking that he should like to make plenty of money which he might then spend on good enterprises. But business left him cold, and he decided that he would go to Oxford.

Oxford is, of course, a world in itself, with its glorious old spires, its ancient halls and its cheerful young spirits everywhere. For a man with imagination here is a good place to see his life and his generation in perspective, and to take some soundings of himself and the needs of his age. Into its full life he threw himself without reserve, making many good friends, drinking in much intellectual and literary stimulus, and finding no small place for himself in his own college, where he was captain of boats during his third year.

A flexibility of spirit enabled him to live his career in two compartments socially. In the company of what the English call the " hearty " (the good fellows, the athletes, the happy-go-lucky), he was a " hearty," too: and in the company of the pious (whom the English call " pi "), he could be " pi " also. These two sets of friends represented two real sides of his nature: he liked this world and felt at home in it, and yet he believed also in the other and believed that it had something to say to us here and now. But he had never found a synthesis between these two sides of him: his life was divided. " I was desperately afraid that one of my two sets of friends might find out my allegiance to the other," he says. He tells me that the religious activities of the place seemed to him " extraordinarily mild," and that his real attitude toward the organized side of them was blasé. " The good Christians offered no challenge. It was perfectly possible to run with the hare and hunt with the hounds."

One summer he went to Keswick for the great conference which also draws many undergraduates. There he ran foul of Frank Buchman, Sherwood Day and others, and this is his impression of them: " They and the people who moved and worked with them instantly challenged me by the quality of their lives and the effectiveness of their work. I saw them only at intervals; and between times, while I knew in my heart they were right, I criticized them behind their backs because I refused to face in my own life the problem which they incarnated for me of absolute surrender to Christ with all its implications." Keswick was one of these intervals. F. B. felt led to win this man, and one morning came face to face with him on the street, and there followed a growingly real relationship and a strengthening of ties which were later to be very close.

In the summer of 1924, a group of six of us set sail for a world-journey. It was to be a training-time for us in working in a fellowship. Jesus seems to have taught His disciples how to work by taking them with Him in small companies, and showing them how to lay siege to definite situations, whether individuals, or towns: it was to show them principles by action. Some of us have come to believe that the greatest need in deepening the spiritual currents of modern Christianity is a small group of completely committed men, committed to Christ first, and then committed unbreakably also to one another in abiding fellowship which has all things in common. This cannot be had for the asking, and its rarity explains the disintegration of many an attempted spiritual movement. The travelling fares were costly, but they were nothing to the expense in patience, honesty and love which welded that inner group. A great deal was accomplished in various missionary centres and colleges, and we are still in touch with many whom we met on that trip. But probably the deepest result of that journey lies in our relationship to one another, in learning to function in a team at all, in discovering how to play second fiddle and yet take real leadership, and in finding that the diversity of gift and personality, once it is possessed by " the same Spirit," produces a much richer and more rounded effect than the usual efforts of one great personality functioning alone. Such a trip is far from easy. Frank Buchman was the leader of it: he is a magnificent traveller, a great companion, an amazing opener of apparently closed doors: but we were not off on a pleasure-jaunt, he took us to train us, and he did his job. The rough edges, the small selfishnesses, the want of spiritual imagination, the disguised wilfulnesses and independences had to go, and in the going pride got crucified more than once. Not many religious leaders have the courage or the imagination to take six grown men apart for several months, treat them like spiritual children, if such they are, and ripen them into spiritual maturity and leadership, till they can be counted on. The fellowship which was

bought at high cost that year has not faltered. Most
of us have come back to take up leadership in various
centres, and through it all, the closest of all human
ties has been the Fellowship. " During that year,"
says the College Chaplain, " the decision was fully
made which should have been made years before, and
which services and meetings and conventions failed to
bring about—the decision to do God's will at any cost.
I knew the meaning of surrender long before I surrendered. It eventually came as a result of continued
exposure to the challenging influence of the team in
the situations where we found ourselves during those
months abroad. In an old bungalow in Madras came
also the conviction that it was full-time Christian
work for me, and the ministry. I look upon that year
round the world, apart from its broadening vision, as
the time of my greatest spiritual development and
growth."

On his return to England, there followed his course
in theological college. For a man whose religious
experience is hazy, a theological seminary can be a
pretty unhappy place: he is called upon to anatomize
something which he does not much understand, and
it may die on the dissecting table while he is cutting it
up. Most seminaries assiduously cultivate " the devotional life," and that is a helpful offset to undiluted
intellectual activity. But something else is needed,
too: a real experience of the Christ a man is to preach,
moral victory within, and a chance to help people.
Active work needs to be woven in with theoretical
information, just as students of surgery need to see
and take part in operations as well as to hear about
them. Much preoccupation with the merely organizational side of religious work can steal a man's time

away from his studies, and distract him from his purpose: but to be vitally in contact with a few individuals whom one is trying to draw to Christ tones up all his study and his devotional life. Many a man I know could have been saved a bad case of spiritual indigestion if he could have been helped to combine his studies and a constant redemptive touch with a few people. The kind of experience which this man had had gave him a sense of what was really vital in his theological course, and he says, "As a result of all that had gone before, theological college was a time of happy spiritual growth. I saw where knowledge fitted in and helped to interpret experience. Living a life surrendered to Christ gave a sense of His power in work with individuals. Dealing with people was a touch-stone for what I was learning, and helped to throw light on what might otherwise have been purely academic."

Since that time he has been ordained and called to be the chaplain of a college where he is getting at the lives of individual men.

" During his last year in college, a chap was introduced to me who seemed to me an extraordinarily balanced fellow on the outside, but I found him all at sixes and sevens inside. He came to see me afterwards, and asked how he might help a friend of his in desperate need. I found him almost immediately responsive with his mind to the deepest message of the Fellowship, that if we want to change others, we must live the quality of victorious life in Christ ourselves first. But while he knew this, he proceeded to try to help his friend without himself being changed, and he misfired, which made him pretty miserable. He came to a house-party and said little, heard much about surrender but did nothing—he was hedging at the problem of life-work, and therefore could not wholeheartedly give himself to God. Humanly we kept in touch; I saw a lot of him, played with him a lot, and also gave him a chance to see people who were really living with Christ as the centre. He was popular in college, and ran lots of societies, but it was all humanly directed, and he became more and more conscious of his need for God's help. I got him to another house-party, and there daylight seemed to dawn. He has been helped by being included in some of the more advanced sessions: he is an engineer, and he likes to ' see the wheels go round '—this has intrigued him and convinced him. The other day came a letter from him which contained this: ' You and A. have made life not only more real for me, but more bearable during a rather rotten time. . . . Through you and what you have given me, I want to help these friends of mine whom I have sought to help so unsuccessfully in the past. . . . I had sought some meaning in religion, but the chapel services at school and at ———— seemed to preclude the possibility of their being any God. So my religion drifted and I drifted till I felt I could not honestly face the communion ever. But now you have brought reality into it, and into life, and I do thank God here and now for what He has done through you.'

" Then there was a chap at theological college with me. We met one night at a religious meeting in a college room. Though he was an ordinand, he was the sort that delights to break up the religious atmosphere of the meeting, and keep it on either an intellectual or purely human level with spiritual power left out. After this meeting, he carefully avoided me.

I wrote a note, asking him to come in and see me, which ' jarred ' him, but he kept avoiding me. Slowly by friendliness his confidence was won, and guidance came to take further initiative with him. I asked him to meals, went to football matches with him, was interested in the things he liked. There developed a growing sense of dissatisfaction and lack in him. He knew that he had strong likes and hatreds of people, that he had a sharp and cruel tongue, that he was proud and superior, and that although he was headed for the ministry, he had no conviction, no message, and no real vocation as yet. While away during Christmas vacation, I was led to write him frankly and deeply: humanly I feared the possible effect of this letter. When we got back to college, he began to take the initiative with me, and called frequently. One morning came guidance to put to him a deep challenge, to tell him that he needed to surrender all to Christ, and that very evening in the firelight in my room, I put the challenge to him fully, frankly and unavoidably. There we had a time of Quiet, during which I was led to pray aloud for him: then more silence—and at last he gave himself to Christ that night, and told Christ so aloud. There has been great fellowship since, and I began to take him further steps and prepare him for those probable returns of the Old Adversary with seven more like himself—(and he brought them, all right!). But we had daily Quiet Times together. At a house-party and in college he began to witness for Christ. His friends noticed the change in his life, his manner, his tongue: swearing and hate went, and a Celtic temperament became divinely controlled under the Holy Spirit. Now he has begun definitely to win others for Christ. He has a life-changing message: love for those he hated, discipline where he was at loose ends. His friends wonder at him. He is convincing." So often it is these headstrong men who go out into the ministry to be the *enfants terribles* of the Church, the scoffers at the supernatural, the enemies of true religion, because back in seminary nobody nipped their egotism in the bud and met their deepest needs.

Quietly he goes on turning friendships to spiritual account in the college where he works.

V

THE FINDING OF A SELF

IF any man knows within him deep, unresolved, unhealed divisions which cleave his life into unrelated segments, and wants unification beyond all other things, here is a story which will help him if only I can tell it aright.

I first met the man of whom I am writing when he had not been long out of college. He was spare and tall, and seemed a mixture of immaturity and ripeness. His Phi Beta Kappa key flashed like a tiny but sharp sword tied to his watch-chain. I knew his father, who is a bishop: and I was struck by a certain ill-at-ease quality in the son which was in striking contrast to the exceptional serenity of his father. I had no idea at the time that we would be thrown later into the closest of working intimacy, or that there were the deep needs and profound rifts in his life of which he told me afterwards.

He had been brought up in this minister's family, one of three happy children. His father has been adored by every congregation he has served, as he is now by his diocese: and his mother has spent herself unsparingly for her family,—a very human Christian. The idealism of high school days included mammoth expectations of rather vague service to humanity.

But college brought its special problems for this sensitive lad from a mid-western city, consciously a minister's son, finding himself in a new and very wide world, where the old atmosphere of religion was forgotten. "Religion was not the thing at college," he says: "there were religious activities on the campus, but they were not represented by the fellows I wanted to know. My old childhood dream about following in father's steps gave way. The practical meaning of what I was getting was materialism: to make money, to be at home in the things of this world seemed to me the only practical thing to do." He said his prayers by rote sometimes, but for the most part they were relegated to the scrap-heap with the old ideals which went with them. He buried himself pretty thoroughly in the amusements and dissipations which many collegians enjoy, and which were so deliciously different from what he had known before.

When it was over, the old problem of life-work met him. Nothing else had made a serious bid for his attention. He knew the family would like him to go into the ministry, and accordingly he told them that he would make a stab at it.

"In this frame of mind," he says, "I found myself at a seminary. The very first day I was there, I met a member of the Fellowship, while I was wandering around disconsolately, rather rueful at the thought of spending a trial year in this place: I liked his jovial attractiveness. The same day came five others; and in those first months as I began to catch in their lives a glad seriousness of purpose about Jesus Christ, I came to think that there was perhaps a lot more in Christianity than I had realized. They were not the sort of men I expected to find in a seminary, and I wondered what had gotten them interested. They tried to make clear to me what it was that had made them give up their obvious prospects of worldly success and go into the ministry. I wanted to see the particular crowd of people who had sent to the seminary so interesting a bunch of friends."

One week-end a meeting was held for half a dozen men from his seminary, and they brought him along. "It was an utterly novel and fascinating experience to me," he says, "to see this attractive circle of men intent on finding God's will. It was there that I first met the idea of ' guidance.' Frank Buchman explained it to us. I remember now sitting in that circle with everyone quiet, and a few of them writing things on scraps of paper. My own mind was an utter blank, but I could not help thinking that to listen to God must be as natural as to pray to Him. There seemed to me to be in that crowd a real understanding of the deepest problems of life. I had had for some years in my own life problems which I had never been able to solve. I decided to talk them over with one of the men, and did. From that week-end, I knew that the only life to live was a guided life, centred in Jesus Christ. I knew that it would mean victory and release. I decided at all costs to find it for myself. All that summer I searched for it amongst books, amongst all kinds of people, but somehow I did not find it."

In his middle year, he came to a house-party. This is what he says: "Thoroughly beaten in my efforts to find God, disgusted with myself for my failures and with the world in general, I was ready to quit religion. The house-party nettled me. Their talk of God was so much bunk, and I decided to throw the whole business overboard and get into business for myself. Then I happened to hear a man telling a few of his friends gathered about him of how real God was in his life.

Somehow the quiet assurance of what he said got under my skin, and I believed it. Just then, with a flash of new life, there stole through my whole being an overwhelming and illuminating experience of God's presence. The two months following were the richest days of my life thus far. They were bathed in the splendour of knowing God. Guidance was clear. Witness was spontaneous. People made decisions."

"Then," he goes on, "God began to ask me to give up cigarettes—not, I imagine, for the cigarettes' sake only, but for what they symbolized of self-indulgence, of masculine compensation for inferiority, of comradeship with the interesting pagan friends at home. They seemed such a little thing: why must they go? Yet the conviction persisted that they must. And as I delayed, and refused by delaying, the vision faded. The experience of God which had been real for two months was gone, gone because I would not take the further steps involved in it, especially the step of thorough discipline on self-indulgence. For two years I constantly vacillated between an enthusiasm for Christ, and a grim determination that I would shake myself free and live the pagan life up to the hilt."

During this time, he had graduated from the seminary, and been ordained to the diaconate. I invited him to come to us as an assistant. This is what he says about it: "In some ways I wanted to come to Calvary, but in other ways I was afraid. I knew that it involved coming down off this fence where I had sat teetering for two years, and making an utter commitment of my life to Christ's highest standards for me. I took three months off for vacation before I was going to assume my work, arriving on the job the day after Labour Day. I felt the terrible pressure, not of any one person, but of the situation itself. Perhaps it was the pressure of the Holy Spirit to make that absolute commitment from which I was running away. I wanted to take refuge in a decent life such as being an architect, anywhere else than where I had to face such a relentless claim as Christ was making. I would not face the pressure, and I could not stand it, so I ran away, went back home and told the family I could not endure working in Calvary Church."

At this time I was still away on my vacation, where I received from him a letter which I quote verbatim: " I arrived here for work, or Lord knows what, today. I would have written you long ago if I could have, but I haven't yet reached a settled and serene frame of mind in which to do it: so here goes, anyway. I can't do this job for you this coming year. God knows, I'd like to; just for your sake. But what you want done can't be done for your sake. The flare-up of conversion experience that I went through the first of August was merely a flash in the pan. It burnt out the last bit of religious fervour that I had left in me. Since then there has been always one recurrent thought in the back of my mind: ' I'm fed up and through with the whole G—— d—— business of religion.' That is all I can think of: just those words. That's the theme of my attitude. I'm sorry as the very devil, Sam; but I can't help it, or I refuse to help it. So I will get out now; or wait till your return, and then get out. I'm a thousand times more hardened than I ever was before; but I will have to put up with it. Sincerely,———"

Two days later came another: " I suppose my last was somewhat foolish and hysterical; but I meant and still mean what I said. I feel I must leave, and I am leaving now. . . . —— suggested that I have a ' surrender inhibition,' which describes the situation pretty well. I don't mean to let myself off with a psychological phrase. For I know as well as you do that surrender inhibitions are basically due to fear or self-love, or Lord knows how many wrong motives. That is, sin. It seems to me now in a sane moment that it is a form of mental unbalance that I will have to get rid of by indirection. So I am planning to get off in a small church of my own, if I can get one, and work like blazes, and forget for a while the whole business of surrender. If I can't get one, I shall go into business and not worry about the consequences. I am sorry to turn out such a flat tire on you. It would be a satisfaction to do the heroic thing; both because it would please you, and because everybody likes to be a hero; but it is impossible at the present time."

It seems to me that there are three fatal things to do with a man in such a frame of mind as this: the first is to smooth it over, pretend that it is minor, and refuse to let the moral pus out of his system; the second is to be discouraged or disgusted with him, and say that after such a long time and so much blowing hot and cold he ought . . . etc.; the third is to push him and take advantage of the extreme uncertainty and suffering and force your own will upon him. He needs to be surrounded by love and allowed to work out his own half-salvation and see with his own eyes that it is incomplete. " Finally, after a month of hesitation," he tells me, " of depression, and after a long time of prayer with my Father, I decided to try the ministry and see what would happen. I got a job as assistant in a large parish, and spite of all that was done for me from without, I was miserable within from the word go. It put me in the hypocritical posi-

tion of preaching a Christian Gospel which I knew in
my heart of hearts I had run away from. The job at
Calvary was always held open for me, with confidence
that some day I would come around. Six months of
that inward conflict was enough. I gave up the other
job and came to Calvary. What a weak and broken
reed I was, I need not remind you."

He continues: " Those first three weeks at Calvary
were, I think, the hardest weeks I ever spent in all my
life. Everywhere I turned I found people fully committed to Christ. I went down to Calvary Mission
and got the full impact of that work: if drunks and
bums had given their all to Christ and been remade,
who was I to hold out on Him? Yet in spite of this
terrific invisible pressure which I felt coming upon me
through the staff at Calvary, everyone was kindness
itself. The person who impressed me most in those
three weeks was one of the girls on the staff. Her
sweeping, lavish, daring surrender to Christ fascinated
me. There was a breezy, romantic quality in it which
lured me and I wanted to know the secret of it. One
Wednesday morning she told me that the secret of her
life lay in an experience of the atoning Cross of Christ.
That morning I realized for the first time in my heart
what had before been only words, the marvellous self-
giving love of Christ, and the caddish shamefulness of
my own weakness and self-love. I surrendered everything on my knees that morning, and I meant it. I
was ready to die for Christ. From that day on life
has been utterly different."

Two days later came his ordination to the priest-
hood. It set a seal to this new inward experience. A
quiet assurance has taken the place of his faltering
uncertainty. Inner victory clothed itself in the gar-

ment of outer radiance. All of us knew that something transforming had happened to him at last. Nearly four years of backing and filling, interest and revulsion, and at last the unification of the divided personality, the emergence of his true aim and ideal, the finding of a self. Now and then, in the blatant sinner, you will get a sudden and complete change, a clean break with his past which cuts his life into two; but it is much more rare to see a man full of inward conflicts, bothered by subtler and more complex difficulties of attitude and adjustment, come to such an abrupt and certain period in his old life, and begin the new with such assurance and finality. That is more than two years ago. Like all of us, he has faced his battles and undergone his temptations: but never have I seen a shadow cross his face which meant that he was looking back on the old life. He has found a long, swinging stride in his work. He has married a girl who lives upon a guided basis with him, and herself has found release in Christ and great joy in witnessing simply with people for Him. He has developed a most unusual power of diagnosis, and can get behind false defenses and down to the real trouble with people in less time than most people I know. And as I write, he is off upon a mission in South Africa, where he will work principally with university men: and I can see him puncturing intellectual pride, and touching those men where they really live. This message tears such a thick sham from off the face of life!

In the parish where he stayed for those six divided months, was a young man who had charge of the boys' club. " He was clean-cut, happy-go-lucky, and married. His chief pride was a second-hand car he owned,

and a plot of camping ground near the Delaware
Water Gap, whither he made tracks every week-end.
He worked during the week in the office end of an
elevator factory.   He had never had more than a
grammar-school education.   One night he and his wife
asked me to dinner with them in their apartment.
Afterwards his wife had other things to do, and he
and I talked till late into the night—talked about
everything under the sun, inconsequentially—the elevator business, the camp, the exciting memories of
his life.   Then we got down to the boys' club.   What
was he doing for it?   Did he know what their real
problems were?   Was he spending all his time getting
a point of contact, and then never using it?   Did he
know how to win a boy's confidence?   I shared what
mine had been at their age, and told of problems
which had dogged my way all through college and
seminary, and how finally I had found a victorious
solution in the power of an experience of Christ.
My sharing made us face our deepest needs together.
In those mighty, unseen currents, running deep below
the surface of life, we found ourselves alike.   Here he
was, a leader among boys, doing everything for them
in the way of recreation and sports, but utterly failing
to touch their deepest moral and spiritual needs, because he himself had always been a person whose
needs were unmet.   He asked the way out.   We talked
of surrender and guidance, and finally about midnight we knelt down and gave our lives anew to God
together.   He found that night a new life of power
and vision.   He told his wife.   At first she almost
resented this sudden acquisition of spiritual power
and joy, but since she has come to find it for herself,
and she has been greatly daring in the way she has

shared it, and has been wonderfully used in helping
people."

One day while he was at Calvary a Methodist minister came in to see me. He had heard of lives being
changed through the work here, and he wanted to
know about it first-hand. I was busy with someone
else, and I sent him to the senior assistant. " I was
horribly immature looking," says the latter, " and I
appeared to be enthusiastic. Both things he disliked.
And he disliked being palmed off on a curate. He
was monosyllabic with me. I did not know whether
to say good-bye, or to try to interest him. Guidance
came to tell him of six months of failure in my last
job, the hell of compromise in preaching a victorious
message because I was officially committed to it, when
I was utterly defeated in my own life. He understood that and grew interested, and wanted to know
how it had worked out. I told him of the constant
challenging patience of the people at Calvary, of how
my commitment had come three weeks after coming
here, the irrevocable discarding of my self-indulgences,
and the decision to live a transparent sharing life.
' That is what I must have,' he said. He had a church
filled with bickering and jealousy; he was preaching a
Gospel he believed to be true, but so far he had not
been able to verify it in his own personal experience.
We knelt down together, oblivious to the difference in
our age and length of service, and the age-old miracle
of the grace of God was again made manifest. Since
then he has found the spiritual message that has
meant healing in a divided church, and preaching
which has been not in word only but in power."

At the end of two years of service here at Calvary,
he wrote me thus: " I cannot forbear to write you a

word of personal gratefulness on the completion of two years at Calvary. They have been rich years, and I am grateful to God for them: the grounding in discipline which has been given, the wealth of fellowship, the silent vicarious absorbing of the mistakes of my own sin, and blindness and inadequacy, the patient waiting for me to grow, the gift of my wife, and the marvellous year we have had together, the increasing vision that God has been giving in the last month about what the Fellowship may mean to the world. . . . So often I lose my vision and get in the grip of the commonplace: I pray God to keep me always true to His first plan. I am sometimes stabbed with fear when I think how narrowly I missed walking into deflective and second-best plans of life. The angle of difference between a good human ministry and a supernatural Gospel is not very great when you are at the point of the angle. Most deeply of all I am convinced that the only salvation for our suicidal civilization lies in a fellowship of men who are utterly dominated and led by the Holy Spirit."

" My experience with the Fellowship," he continues, " has really made the ministry for me a possible career. Without it I should have had to go ahead as a hypocrite, preaching one thing and living another. That I could not have done for long: somewhere I should have gone on the rocks, shattered my life completely, or else steeled myself to money-making or pleasure. Thank God the chance was allowed me to commit my will to Christ on that priceless day of final decision in that spiritual matrix of absoluteness for Christ which we call Calvary Church. Increasingly my life has been unified around Him. Slowly He is claiming area after area in my life for Himself—family, friends, pleasures, the physical side of life, the desire for power. It has been painful, but it has been rich. And I have learned from the Fellowship also not to think of my life in terms of a job done, a tangible stint of human work accomplished, but rather in maintaining a certain quality of life that is given of God, a ' being ' much more than a ' doing,' which of course proves to be actively redemptive as it flows its way along. All accomplishment ought to issue as a by-product of living that quality of life with God. The job is no longer to sit down and puzzle out what I can do to serve most deeply my fellow-men: but to discover God's picture for my life, and where He feels it needs to tie in with the lives of others. The world of the ministry for me is the individual. That individual's relation to God, and his redemptive relation to others is the real task of a minister. How to relate him on the deepest levels to his God and his neighbour—this is what the message of the Fellowship has taught me. This limiting the field of one's work increases its depth. I know now that it is my job to propel forth into the world contagious units for God, being convinced that three lives contagious for God will leaven the whole lump far more quickly and far more truly than a crowd of church-goers."

VI

JOCULATOR DOMINI

I SUPPOSE that the rarest people in the world are the spiritually merry. One comes upon quantities of people who go far enough in their religion to be earnest, but few who go far enough to be glad. Many a serious life carries on, within and without, a splendid and brave warfare against the things of darkness, and in behalf of the things of light: but not many there are who find in this warfare something akin to a very high form of sport. And yet the quality which I mean is much profounder than the hilarity and animal spirits of sport: it is much more like what a man feels when he has been saved from a shipwreck than what he feels when he has broken the world's record throwing a discus. For the heart of spiritual merriment is gratefulness, not accomplishment: it is the blessedness of God's mercy, not satisfaction with one's own character.

When the Dark Ages were done, the day dawned, and Francis of Assisi was the sun. He fitted no categories of holy men, and the people called him God's merry-maker, the Joculator Domini. If you want to understand all that is involved in that term, you must read G. K. Chesterton's life of St. Francis. I am borrowing the phrase to apply to a modern English gentleman of thirty-five, a minister of the Church of England, because the most signal thing about him is a kind of radiance which is as far as possible from professional religious cheerfulness, and which seems to me the perfect outward index to his own deep inward joy in Christ.

He went to one of the English public schools, where he entered whole-heartedly into the life, and was a keen sportsman. While there he was confirmed after being prepared " en masse " by the Headmaster. " The preparation was careful," he says, " but failed to get across to most of us. It was too intellectual and too impersonal. The problems common to most of us, such as impurity and dishonesty, were never met. On the day before confirmation, we lined up outside the Head's study, awaiting our interview. When my turn came, I was asked if I had any problems, to which, of course, I replied, ' No,' and was allowed to leave after being given a little prayer card upon which was printed some excellent advice. Confirmation made little or no vital impression on my life. My religion at that time was that of the typical English public school boy, that is, it meant being a good sportsman and playing the game. There was a certain code of honour, but it came very short of Christ's standard. I enjoyed the chapel services chiefly because I loved to sing in the choir. I listened attentively to the Head week by week, but his sermons never got under my skin. Prayer certainly meant something, but it was chiefly concerned with requests that one might win one's cricket or soccer colours, or else an urgent S.O.S. for help out of a scrape.

"After school I went to a country on the Continent to learn the language, lived with a family there, and first began to come up against the darker side of life. I was disgusted with the undreamt of baseness and immorality, even in young adolescents of both sexes: I wanted to help them, and stand up for the ideals which had unconsciously formulated themselves through the influence of home and school. But I felt impotent to make much impression.

"Then I chanced to attend a Confirmation Service conducted by the Bishop of Northern Europe in the little English Church in ———. During that service something happened which changed my whole outlook. It wasn't so much what was being done or said, but that in the stillness suddenly the living Christ became a wonderful reality for the first time. This was my conversion, and there is little doubt in my mind that it was an answer to my mother's prayers. I was always happy before, but I left that church radiant and overflowing with new life. There was a sense of inward peace and power, and that now one had something to give to those in spiritual need.

"I hadn't long to wait. I was now a voluntary clerk in a local insurance company, working in order to gain experience. Many a time another clerk would say that he would like to have what he saw I got from my religion. I was once asked to talk very informally to several of my brother clerks, and though I had not been long in the country the words were given and an impression made. Shortly after, one Saturday night, when one of them was celebrating his betrothal, and the party was about to break up and visit the local brothels, I appealed to them to stand by me and go straight to their homes. They wavered, and I knew it was not easy to break the habit of years, but all except one of the party of thirty lined up with me, and a night of debauchery was avoided, and in a few lives a new ideal was born.

"After nearly a year's absence, I returned to England to join my father's firm in London. This began for me a short period of backsliding, due chiefly to my inability to adapt myself to the restricted life at home. Abroad everything and everyone were so delightfully unconventional, and at home there seemed to be such an artificial air about most people. The Church was dull and lifeless, and the lack of anything spiritual to do was my chief reason for slipping. This period of drift was checked by the frank challenge of a girl, later destined to be my wife, who was the first person ever to hold me to the highest. Soon after she left for Canada, but her influence remained."

He then made a change to another company of underwriters and insurance brokers to gain a wider experience. The Chief, who was an outstanding Christian, told him in his first interview that the firm was a big family, all pulling together, and taught him, he says, "the immense value of teamwork and mutual trust, which later played such a big part as a soldier of Britain and more particularly as a soldier of Christ." He tells me also that during this time lives were touched for Christ, both in the office and socially at home, and some were definitely won: but that he was "still conscious of an inadequacy to meet their deepest needs." That phrase is worth using as a spotlight to turn upon our religious work.

"Then came the Great War," he goes on. "As in business, so as a soldier, I threw myself into it wholeheartedly. The war years probably saw the greatest development of my character. I joined up in the Inns of Court O.T.C., received a Commission in the Royal Sussex Regiment, and three months after went to

France as a second lieutenant on active service. On my first leave, I was married. I was promoted captain, commanding a company in three different battalions. After the Armistice I marched into Germany with the First Division, and remained six months with the Army of Occupation.

" During these army days, two outstanding incidents influenced my career.

" Just before the Third Battle of Ypres, in which we as a battalion were to take part, the men clamoured one Sunday for a service. No padre being available, a Y. M. C. A. secretary who knew that I cared about religion asked me to hold a voluntary service for the brigade. Somehow the news got round that a Sussex officer was going to take a service in the evening, and long before it was time to start, the hut was crowded out, men were hanging round the windows and the doors, eager to catch a word. We sang the old favourite hymns, and then I spoke to them very simply about my Best Friend, Jesus Christ, and why I did not fear death. The Holy Spirit fell upon us, and many a decision was made to take Christ into one's life. Possibly in many cases this was due to the uncertainty of the immediate future, but it was none the less sincere, as the following story will show.

" Some weeks later, during the attack on Paschendael, a brother officer and his runner were cut off by heavy shell fire. As they lay in a shell hole, scarcely expecting to survive the barrage, the officer enquired whether the little fellow, a mere lad of nineteen, was afraid of death. ' No,' he said, ' but I was until one Sunday when the battalion was out at rest just before the thirty-first of July show at Ypres, and then I heard one of our officers tell why he was not afraid of death, and since then somehow life has just been different. I have no fear now, for Christ is always near me.'

"Another incident, possibly connected with the first, occurred some months later. As they had done long ago in a business office, some of my men wanted to know more about my religion. They thought they could catch it by being confirmed, and asked the brigade padre what could be done about it. He was one of the very best, and had already won a Military Cross with Bar for conspicuous bravery. Knowing what I stood for, he put up to me that I should prepare my own men for confirmation. At first I was taken aback, and told him I was not a padre, but just a soldier. 'True,' he said, 'but you are also a soldier of Jesus Christ. Tell them simply what He means to you.' Accordingly, at my next opportunity, when the battalion was out at rest, my confirmation class was begun. It comprised a sergeant, a lance corporal, and eight privates. We met some dozen times, and these talks have since formed the basis of my confirmation talks, as an ordained parson. They had to be practical and real, and so they probably got across better than the lectures I had received as a boy. My candidates were duly confirmed, and it did seem to make a very real difference, not only to them, but to the whole battalion.

" These incidents, and innumerable talks with officers and men, gave one the longing to minister to them in civilian life, if ever the war ended and one came through alive. But all my training had been to take over my father's business and carry on the name as the eldest son. Then, too, I was married, and there was not enough cash to buy one's own home and get trained as a padre. The thing was impossible. Yet the idea persisted!

"Then two strange things happened.

"One evening, just after the Armistice, I unexpectedly ran into one of my subalterns in Vaux Andiney, a small shattered village just behind the old German line. We sat over the dying embers of a fire in a ruined cottage. Our conversation turned on the future. Before the war he had been up at Magdalen College, Oxford, and was hoping to return for a short while before ordination. 'Why, old man,' he said, 'you know you ought to come up to Oxford, too, and get ordained—you are just the kind of fellow that is wanted.' 'Nonsense,' I said, 'I loathe parsons, and besides I am a business man, and I am certain Christian men are needed just as much in business as in the ministry, if not more. Then, too, there isn't a living wage in the Church for a married man. It's impossible.' But the thought rankled. I talked it over with my wife, and we felt it was out of the question, placed as we were. We made our plans for me to return to business on my next leave. We bought a little house near London, and furniture, and all was in readiness for the happy day when the demobilization order should come through. At last, in April, 1919, it came.

"On the way to the train in Cologne, the thought came to go and inquire at the Chaplain's Department about the conditions of training for the ministry. To my surprise, as I entered the door, there stood my old brigade padre. 'Whatever brings you here?' I asked: 'I thought you had got a Blighty a year ago.' 'So I had,' he replied, 'but here I am back, as you see, and strangely enough I have come here today to put the authorities on to you as a possible candidate for Holy Orders.' I said, ' Good heavens, padre, it is an amazing world: I have just come here myself to make enquiries about the very same thing.' Needless to say, every faculty was given, and after a delightful interview with the Chaplain General in London, and innumerable difficulties and delays overcome, I found myself in Oxford as an undergraduate in October, 1919, reading Honours Theology with a view to entering the Anglican ministry. Almost the first person I met at Oxford was my subaltern friend from Magdalen, who was not a little surprised that our chance talk round the fire at Vaux Andiney had had such momentous consequences for me.

"After three happy years up at Oxford, I took my degree and was ordained to a curacy in Sussex."

It was during the summer of 1922 that the Joculator Domini first came into touch with the First Century Christian Fellowship. With a number of other men from Oxford, he was attending the Keswick Convention, beside one of England's loveliest lakes. " One evening," he goes on, " there came to supper a visitor from the U. S. A. Afterwards he stayed and conducted prayers in the most delightful and informal manner. He began by just getting acquainted with the party, and suggested they should tell him anything of general interest about themselves. Then he talked for a short while, and this was followed by a period of silence. For many it was the first ' living silence ' they had ever experienced, and very different from a ' dead silence.' The visitor was Frank Buchman, and two days later several members of the party were meeting with him and others for a Quiet Time every morning at seven o'clock. It was a new and wonderful experience. In those Quiet Times illuminating thoughts were given to many, inspired by the Holy Spirit of God. These for the most part were intimately related to the practical affairs of everyday life.

"Very soon some of the party recognized in this Fellowship something unique in their experience. Here were believing units of many different churches and countries, making up a living organism but without organization. Membership was based solely upon the relationship of the individual to the risen Lord and Master. Further investigation proved that they stood for nothing new, but a simple belief in the New Testament and the application of its message to life in the twentieth century. Old truths, however, were being emphasized in a new and vital way. The whole atmosphere was so joyous and natural that it compelled attention. It was not long till some of that party were wholehearted and enthusiastic supporters of what they discovered to be a movement for vital religion within the churches. Of that first company, one is now a chaplain and fellow of a college in Oxford University, a second is a chaplain in Cambridge, and a third is doing pastorate work among university and public school men.

"What did touch with this movement do for me? For the first time in my life I found myself challenged by a group of people who would not take me for granted. Never before had I seen people who would share themselves with one in absolute honesty, and deal with one's sins. Though I had been converted to Christ many years before, they made me face up for the first time to His fourfold challenge of absolute honesty, purity, unselfishness and love. For years I understood the meaning of consecration, but had not been fully consecrated. This Fellowship was used of God to make me wholehearted.

" Twice Frank Buchman travelled from London to Sussex to see me. On the second of these visits, he held me to the very best, and showed me that without adequate discipline, my life could never be one hundred per cent effective. Through the long Quiet Times which he recommended, I discovered four things which needed putting right in my life:

1. There was one person who had wronged me whom I would not forgive.
2. There was a restitution which I would not make.
3. There was a doubtful pleasure which I would not give up.
4. There was a sin in the long past which I would not confess.

When these were straightened out, I not only came into new power and release, but for the first time began to get daily guidance which I knew could be relied and acted upon, because my own life was disciplined. Almost daily new surrenders have to be made, but I can honestly say that nothing is left standing between God and myself, or other people and myself. Consequently, I entered upon a period of radiant joy and peace, and life is just wonderfully full and overflowing.

"As the years passed my interest in the work of the Fellowship increased, but for a long time whilst I was in full sympathy I was really running and working parallel to them, and not wholly within. Recently I have seen the implications of team-work as opposed to individual effort, and since then the difference in my own life and work has been enormous.

This is much more than merely a question of close co-operation: it gets at certain prides of individuality and subtle dissociation which I had not recognized before. People were helped in the past, but really now it is almost a daily experience for someone in need to be brought, by God's grace, into touch with the Saviour. Through the leading of the Holy Spirit in the Quiet Time one has learned something of the difficult art of soul-surgery, and now can face fearlessly the deepest problems of those who come. After seven years' contact with this group, in Great Britain, Holland, South Africa and the United States, I must say that I have met no group of Christians who have so consistently held me to the highest, or come so near to Christ's ideal. This being so, loyalty to Christ involved loyalty to this Fellowship, not simply as an interested and sympathetic observer, or even co-operator, but as one from within, as a member of the team playing the most romantic game in life. During the last year I have travelled far, and also worked for a long stretch in one place, and experience has in every case proved that only as individuals are welded by the Holy Spirit into a wholehearted team can the best work be done for God. Not only is the impact of a team greater, but individuals are developed to a remarkable degree. There is something invaluable and unique about the depth of fellowship on a guided basis of Christian living, where the members are of one heart and one soul, sharing their deepest convictions as well as their possessions, and having all things common. The wonder and joy of it must be experienced to be believed.

" I want to carry this point about loyalty further. In actual practice, when the life is God-directed, no real loyalties conflict. On the contrary, one's loyalty to his particular branch of the Church, and other Christian organizations, loyalty to wife and family, have all been enhanced; for now behind the individual are the prayers and support of a world-wide Fellowship. When there appears to be a conflict in loyalties, there is want of guidance somewhere, and unsurrender. When it has all been submitted to God, and relationships have been straightened out, the road will be clear.

" I am now ministering to undergraduates. I have found no ' way ' so effective as that advocated by the Fellowship, in dealing with students. In three years some five hundred of them, both men and women, have come of their own accord for personal talks. Many of them had deep needs which I know I could not have met had I not had my own needs met by Frank Buchman, or someone else. Each term several hundred men and women come into our home. It is no uncommon experience to be booked up with interviews, like a doctor or a dentist, a week ahead. In my church, I expect after preaching to have people who want to come along for a talk, and so every facility is given them. This was an experience almost unknown before my touch with the Fellowship group, but now it is the usual thing.

" It is amazing how quickly the corporate Quiet Time, realizing the presence of Christ and seeking to know His mind on the subject under discussion, not only clarifies our thought, but helps to break down all sorts of barriers: and folk who have never spoken in public before find themselves doing it because the atmosphere makes them forgetful of themselves. I have tried this general plan in Teachers' Training

Classes, Bible Classes, and Confirmation Talks, creating an atmosphere of fellowship, and then having a Quiet Time followed by sharing. I know of no other way which is so effective in developing the leadership of even the very young and inexperienced. For instance, two girls under fifteen are working as a team and taking complete charge of a service for children while I am on my vacation. They will be assisted by some half dozen leaders of their own age, but they will give the talks to the children out of their own experience. They were confirmed only last April, and had had no previous experience.

"To sum up, the world and the Church in particular, are hungry for real spiritual fellowship. I know of no better ' way ' to bring this about than the ' way ' of the First Century Christian Fellowship."

VII

RUMOUR AND REALITY

WHENEVER a genuine religious movement gets afoot, two things happen. Some lives are changed, and others are " offended " in the New Testament sense. Again and again, usually from within the body of the Church itself, God has brought forth a man who sees more deeply and dares more profoundly than those about him. In solitude and often in obscurity, he beats out the message he is to deliver, which is the significance for others of his own experience of God. He gathers about him a few believers, slowly, tediously welding them into close fellowship. Then he goes with his message to the world. Religion of this deeper dye goes beneath the surface: it is like a major operation upon the sick body of conventional believers. What goes deep enough to help goes also deep enough to hurt.

Is not this what happened to Jesus Himself? He won a few men to lifelong and martyr's allegiance, and He as inexorably forced others to rank themselves as His enemies, who finally slew Him. The same force was in a sense responsible for both, the force of a clear issue, incarnated in a personality, and calling to men's deepest selves, asking for nothing less than the whole gift of those whole selves. When these were given, there resulted a deathless loyalty: when these were withheld, previous indifference turned often into deadly enmity.

As with the Master, so with the servant. "It is one of the characteristics of the divine word," said John Calvin, "that whenever it appears, Satan ceases to slumber and sleep." Few who know the historic importance of that great body of believers called the Quakers can be anything but thankful to God for plain-spoken George Fox, their founder: yet his *Journal* is full of his warfare against spiritual deadness, and of the retaliation of the ecclesiastical panjandrums, as told in such an incident as this: "A priest opposed while I was declaring the word of the Lord amongst them; for Oliver had several priests about him, of which this was his newsmonger; an envious priest, and a light, scornful, chaffy man. I bid him repent; and he put it in his newspaper the next week that I had been at Whitehall, and had bid a godly minister there repent." The Great Awakening of the eighteenth century in England called the Church back to life, but with what vilification of the Wesleys and George Whitefield! The latter said, "Contempt and I are pretty intimate, and have been so for above twice seven years." In America today are still hundreds of men and women who owe their first genuine touch with God to D. L. Moody: yet it was said by one of Mr. Moody, "Do you want to know the secret of Moody's success? Well, read Barnum's *Humbugs of the World*. Moody is perfect master of the philosophy of that book."

It is all very well to talk about varying methods, and to say that the ways of some of these spiritual innovators were offensive to refined spiritual taste: the condemnation of the critics is that they could not get deeper than their own æsthetic sensibilities, and recognize the manifest presence of the Spirit of God, initiating spiritual movements which would still be blessing the face of the earth long after they were forgotten, with all their nice little tastes and their supercilious judgments.

Such criticism comes principally, but not entirely, from two sources, as Ignatius Loyola found out. The first is the pagan worldlings and sinners, who do not wish to be reminded of the eternal things, because these are upsetting to the enjoyment of the immediate pleasure: they will at almost any cost protect their consciences against an acute challenge, and make all manner of sport of the prophet or evangelist if only by so doing they may make him to appear the fool instead of themselves. The second source of criticism is the religious folk, conventional, unobserving, without a message for other people, unaware of how far the younger generation has wandered from such faith as they imparted, content with a round of pious duties in church, and with kindness which helps but does not cure, and who resent the very evident presumption of any one's questioning whether they have found all there is to be found in the Christian religion. These want to be disturbed no more than the pagans and unbelievers: and to fear they add jealousy towards those who are having genuine spiritual results. These unlovely emotions are habited in garments of spirituality before they appear in public. The Pharisees of old thought they were doing God service. But in perspective, as one looks back through the years, one sees how many of those who thought they were serving God were in fact fighting against Him.

The story which follows concerns a man whose first

knowledge of the work which brought him at last
decisively to Christ, came through rumour spread by
its enemies. I shall let him tell that part of the story
himself.

But first let me say something of his early years.
He says that religion had a natural place in his life as
far back as he can remember. It centred, as probably religion should, in a lovely mother whose natural
climate is the Kingdom of Heaven, and of whom I
heard it truly said recently that she " defined the
word ' lady.' " She taught him about Jesus, and told
him about a spiritual world which, he says, was made
to seem " perfectly natural although very wonderful."
He tells me that he never really revolted against his
early training, as the manner of many is, because it
was not the kind which made one want to revolt. " I
am deeply grateful," he adds, " that I came through
my early years without misconceptions about God
which would have to be torn down and replaced later.
The Christ to whom I committed my life last winter
was the same Christ to whom I prayed as a child. In
a sense I have always felt that I would ultimately give
my life to Him."

The religious world today is full of discouraged
fathers and mothers, who feel that they have failed,
or are failing, with their children, and that they have
not made religion real to them. Some things parents
can do: they can give a child the " makings " of
religious faith, teach him things his mind will not
have to reject later, and above all, let religion make
of *them* happy, cheerful, honest, companionable, un-
wavering people. They cannot make him take it for
himself, save in rare instances: but they can pray, and
put him in touch with others who have the faculty of

helping him, as this man says, to "commit his life to the same Christ to whom he prayed as a child." May I here quote the great Amiel's wisdom upon this point: "The religion of a child depends on what its mother and father are, and not on what they say. The inner and unconscious ideal which guides their life is precisely what touches the child; their words, their remonstrances, their punishments, their bursts of feeling even, are for him merely thunder and comedy; what they worship, this it is which his instinct divines and reflects."

At eleven he was confirmed, and the next year he entered a church school where there was some real religion. He went regularly to confession and to communion. He does not remember when he first began to feel a call to the ministry, but, as usual, this was partially bound up in a personality, this time that of the head-master, for whom his admiration was intense. It occurred to him that he might be laying down his life for Christ in a similar way. He was a busy, happy lad, normally occupied with school interests; and because of his interest in the chapel services he was made Sacristan in senior year, "a position," says he, "to which I did not take eagerly."

With college came some of the readjustments which are common at eighteen or nineteen. It was a new world, and he liked it. He studied an average amount, plunged into Freshman competitions with much success, and made a lot of friends. There was little extra time: a fraction of it he devoted to religion. But there was much about him that was new and interesting and "religion could wait." He said his prayers regularly, and went to Communion irregularly. He was not bored with religion. Life was simply too full at that time to give it much consideration.

He says that " it was at college that I first heard of the activities of certain mysterious characters who were said to be forcing down unwilling throats a form of religion which was known as ' Buchmanism.'* This was called a ' cult,' and was said to be holding house-parties at various times and places for men and women together, where sex was discussed openly. This was the first wind I had of any such movement. It was said that men and women made open confessions, in mixed groups, of all kinds of hidden sin. Emotion, I understood, was encouraged. The purpose of these house-parties was in some way religious, though exactly what they were supposed to lead to was shrouded in mystery. I remember a letter which appeared in the college daily and which denounced house-parties as pernicious: it was signed by an imposing list of campus notables, amongst them the president of the Episcopalian students' society, who happened to be my brother and who I knew had never been to a house-party. These rumours did not impress me very much one way or the other. They provided an interesting topic of conversation, especially since some of the exponents of this outfit were supposed to be ' operating' on our own campus. I passed along such stories as I heard, with additions from time to time. There was, for instance, the story of a ' Buchmanite ' who called on a prominent Senior without an invitation, worked out of him an emotional confession; then left him, saying that he would give him ten minutes in which to decide whether or not he would give his

---

* A name applied by its opponents to A First Century Christian Fellowship, disliked and never used by any of its members.

life to the ministry. I heard that these high-pressure methods had sent more than one man to the infirmary with a nervous break-down. Everybody, so I was informed, was held guilty of some kind of sexual sin by this cult: and they aimed to have everyone wash his dirty linen in public. What this was good for was not explained, though it was the consensus of opinion that the ' operators ' got an emotional kick out of these rehearsals, and that their thirst for confessions was insatiable.

" These stories did fill me with a kind of curiosity. I met some of the men about whom the rumours were circulated, and they seemed to me on the surface quite normal human beings. I was careful not to become too intimate, however, at first, for fear I might be a victim. Everyone laughed and joked about them, and I joined in the general derision, repeating anything I heard. It is always easier to believe the bad about people than the good—it is more fun. About this time there were a bunch of fellows who called themselves, I think, the ' Society for the Propagation of Moral Turpitude,' an idea which amused us mightily: it was humourous, anti-reform, and begun without any real malice, but it helped to develop the growing attitude of suspicion and hatred on the campus by spreading about these lies and uninvestigated stories. Before it was over, this mischievous affair had done a good deal of harm, and might well have been investigated by the authorities who did investigate the secretaries of the college Y. M. C. A. which had come under the leadership of the ' Buchmanites.' During this investigation, an extraordinary lack of incriminating evidence was forthcoming. It was confidently said that there were thirty undergraduates who would give evi·

dence as to having had their privacy invaded and their characters impugned: but none was ever found to testify. The exoneration of the men at the head of the Y. M. C. A. by the investigating committee aroused only passing comment.

"I have often wondered since what it was that made the college so militant against the movement. I am not quite sure just why I criticized. I had kept more or less loyal to my church through college: it was safe and sane, and had a horror of dangerous methods in spreading the Gospel of Jesus Christ. The Episcopal Society, of which I became the head in my graduating year, was respectable and harmless, few people even knew of its existence; but I derived a sense of having done my duty by belonging to it. I think we criticized the movement because of the innate desire of the average young man to be comfortable. We aimed at graduating from college, and securing for ourselves comfortable little jobs, and comfortable little cars, and comfortable little wives, and perhaps a few comfortable little children: and we did not want our comfortable little opinions disturbed. The Gospel of Jesus Christ is not comfortable to the self-centred man. So if we were to remain comfortable we had to justify ourselves in doing so. If we could find something wrong with the men who challenged us to a new life, we should not have to do anything about it. We would have our peace at any price."

A year ago, while I was in England, I was talking with one of Oxford's great Christian psychologists. He knew the movement intimately, and had given us very valuable help. The work has grown widely in the university, and some two hundred and fifty men turned out for the meetings weekly. I said to him that the movement had received very severe criticism in many places, and asked him what he thought it came from. His answer was along these lines:

" That is not hard for a psychologist to answer. In this Fellowship, you ask a man to give his entire life to Christ—nothing less will do. He must either do it, or find some good reason why he should not. Now, if he can find something wrong in the men who brought the issue to his mind, or in the way they presented it, that will let him off. That is where so much criticism comes from." And then he added a most significant thought: " But don't be too much discouraged. Remember that the opposite of love is not hate, but indifference. And when you have got a man's active dislike, you have got his attention." I thought about Saul of Tarsus and his persecutions, and remembered that his opposition was merely an early stage in his conversion.

To come back again to the story, before his college career was over, our friend had thought seriously about the ministry. For a year he fought it off and temporized by teaching in a small-boys' school. During that year he talked occasionally with his old Headmaster, and came to the conclusion that he could not really be happy until he had faced the whole question of religion frankly and given himself a chance to find out if there were any value in it for him. He agreed to go to a seminary for a year, and " try it and myself out." So he went. At first he was aloof and critical. The men looked like the kind of men that turned into the kind of ministers he knew and didn't like. He resolved to stick it out for a year, and satisfy his conscience for all time that he had " looked into religion," and then get out and lead whatever kind of life seemed best to suit his own inclinations and interests.

" It happened, however," he goes on to say, " that almost immediately after my arrival at the seminary, there was a series of meetings carried on by the Fellowship in a near-by city. At the seminary were three men who belonged to the Fellowship, and they gathered me up and took me along. At these meetings I saw at first-hand the people I had heard and talked about at college. The realization came over me that I had been misled about them and about their message and their procedure. It was hard to see how any of the stories I had heard had gained credence or currency. I began to see a quality of honest, shared, defenceless life which contrasted sharply with my own suspicious and self-justifying attitude. Instinctively I knew that I had done nothing for Christ, and that I had not let Him do anything for me. I watched this quality of life in the members of the Fellowship who were at the seminary.

" Then came a series of challenges. The strongest was from a young minister not connected with the Fellowship, but on whom the mark of Christ was unmistakable. One night I laid my life out before him in its ugly reality and, as I talked, saw myself as I really was. We prayed together, and he asked me whether I was going to keep my old self, or give it, with all its hopes and fears, ambitions, likes and dislikes, to Christ to cure. I said that I would give myself to Christ, and on my knees I made a surrender. Within five minutes I had gotten up and retracted everything I had said. But the memory of that failure stayed with me throughout that autumn, and the presence about me of a few men who I knew had taken that step for better or for worse was a constant reminder of my own cowardice.

"After Christmas there was a house-party within striking distance of the seminary. A good many of the students who had felt the challenge of the lives of the same men who impressed me, decided to go. Two days of it found me under real conviction. I had no answer for a man in need, because nothing had yet met the needs in my own life, and I knew it. At the house-party I kept meeting people in whom I found the same quality of life as I had seen at the previous meetings and in the lives of the three men at seminary. But, though I was facing myself more honestly now, I was in terrific fear of losing the direction of my own life, for that was what a true decision for Christ would mean to me. I ran away from the house-party, and spent a miserable day with myself at the seminary. The next day something stronger than myself made me go back again, and within an hour or two of my arrival I had 'let go and let God,' in the presence of a friend who had laid his life alongside of mine and withheld nothing that might help me.

" I can never forget the release that came. It was indeed as if I had been born again. Back at the seminary I began to experience fellowship on the deepest of levels with the men I had admired, but shied away from because of their challenge. God took control of an old, persistent problem, which I had fought with might and main, and it disappeared.

" There was a young man in a small church where I was working who had the same problem as my own. Those of us who were working there had given him friendship and good advice. But it had not cured him. For a long while I kept getting guidance to share with that boy frankly the thing which God had taken out of my life. So I laid myself out openly to him, and he began to believe that if God had done that much for me, perhaps he, too, could be freed from his trouble. It was the first time he had ever told any one what it was. His surrender was thorough and humble, and since that time he has been obviously the victor over his own life. He used to be a retiring weakling, but from the day of his surrender he has gone ahead step by step making himself into a man. The old sense of inferiority crops up now and again, and with it a certain resentment against the world. But slowly confidence is coming. I believe it has been the beginning of his remaking.

" There are lots of moderately sincere young people," he further comments, " in this world who have a general desire to do good. When I went to the seminary I had in the back of my mind a vague feeling that if I were connected with the Church I could do more good in the world than if I were in some other capacity. It took me some time to realize that Jesus Christ never is satisfied with the ' good '—He requires the best. If I was to come up against crying need in human lives and have an answer for that need, the needs of my own life must be met first, down deep where the world does not see. You can't give what you haven't got. It struck me that too many people were missed entirely by good souls who helped superficially with good advice, sympathy and money. I had had help like this, and it had never cured me, and I knew such things never cured anybody else. The men who did the most for me were the men who cared enough to give themselves, their inner lives and experiences, and helped me to face my own true self and carried me through to a solution. There is all the difference in the world.

"Since my surrender I have repeatedly tried the way of compromise in my own life, and each time any power I might have had in other people's lives has disappeared. With these temporary deflections, new issues arise, new surrenders must be made which bring new release and power. I cannot possibly face a life given to the ministry on any other basis than that of literally dying daily to sin. I have got to be willing to do what others did for me, turn my life inside out where it will help anybody else, and to make sure of my own cleansing experience of Jesus Christ day by day, so that a fellow in need can come to me and find through me a real answer to his troubles—a regenerating experience of Jesus Christ. This may bring me into conflict with the average idea of parish work, perhaps, but I do want to put first things first. It is easy to get side-tracked into a life of intense parish activity, with not much sense of direction, and only meagre results. But Jesus Christ came into the world to save sinners, and I believe that that is still His commission to those who have given themselves to Him without reservation."

Ultimately there is no answer to critics and objectors but the old, pragmatic, New Testament measuring-rod of spiritual fruits. I close with part of a letter which John Wesley wrote to Prebendary Church, of St. Paul's, London, who had severely criticized him:

"Let us bring this question into as narrow a compass as possible. Let us go no further as to time than seven years past, as to place than London and the part adjoining, as to persons than you and me, Thomas

Church preaching one doctrine, John Wesley the other. Now then, let us consider with meekness and fear what have been the consequences of each doctrine. I beseech you to consider in the secret of your heart how many sinners you have converted to God. By their fruits we shall know them. By this test let them be tried. How many outwardly and habitually wicked men have you brought to uniform habits of outward holiness? 'Tis an awful thought. Can you instance in a hundred? In fifty? In twenty? In ten? If not, take heed unto yourself and to your doctrine. It cannot be that both are right before God. Consider now (I would not speak, but I dare not refrain) what have been the consequences of even my preaching the other doctrine. By the fruits we shall know those of whom I speak, even the cloud of witnesses who at this hour experience the doctrine I preach to be the power of God unto salvation. The habitual drunkard that was, is now temperate in all things. The whoremonger now flees fornication. He that stole steals no more, but works with his hands. He that has cursed or swore, perhaps at every sentence, has now learned to serve the Lord with fear, and rejoice unto Him with reverence. These are demonstrable facts. I can name the men, with their several places of abode."

VIII

SUFFICIENT GRACE

THE stories in this book would be shallow and incomplete without including one life upon which the shadow of trouble had fallen, and in whom the magnificent experience of conversion to Jesus Christ had to be sustained far from the glamour of energetic activity and steady achievement: in this case, in the quiet of patiently enduring a stubborn and long-time illness. The question may logically be asked whether it is not the exciting activity in which many of these lives are engaged, with its very rewarding reflex upon themselves, in zest, and joy, and bursting health, which in the last analysis holds them to the new life, rather than spiritual forces alone. I sometimes ask myself whether, if I should go blind, or otherwise be laid aside on the shelf and out of the race I might say to myself, " Where is *now* thy God? " But here is a man who has faced all that, who after a brilliant career in college, and with every promise of an exceptional life, in the high-noon of his youth and champing for activity and achievement and the employment of all his powers, has had to wait indefinitely, and to make a life in the midst of delay. The Gospel is nowhere more put to the test than where it must sanctify disappointment, hallow illness, and dignify enforced idleness, till they become veiled sacraments of God's unremitting watchfulness and care. I should feel that this book were jejune and unworthy of the Master who in the midst of His youth went up upon a cross, if it had in it no special message for the disappointed, the frustrated, the temporarily or chronically ill, those who must make the best of a broken life and who would say, with Baron Von Hugel:* " I have myself, all my life, had to coax, and by various circumvendifuges, get my work out of my restive, kittle-cattle machinery;" and if it did not help them to see that what they must perforce lack in quantity of work, they may make up in quality, so that each act may be set like a jewel in the ample gold of recollection and prayer.

He comes of a Christian family, and his early training in religion was thorough. He went always to church with them, and while he was little it was arranged that during the sermon he might draw in a copy-book: then came a birthday after which he was to " put away childish things," and he began to hear things in the sermons which he could take in and remember. There was a venerable pastor, tall and straight in his frock coat, who both awed and interested the children. There is no science accurate enough to take account of all these early impressions: but we know enough to be sure that they heap up in the invisible cellars of memory, and blossom forth later on when the sufficient stimuli are present.

A year before he entered college, he was spending his fourth season in a boys' camp on Lake Champlain. That summer, he says, the surprising thought struck him that religion could be adventurous and deeply attractive. The spirit of the camp was always

* *Letters to a Niece*, Baron Friedrich Von Hugel, p. 81.

one of rare friendliness and fellowship: many are the men that I know upon whom that camp has left an ineffaceable spiritual mark. Suddenly he began to identify the " camp spirit " with the Christian spirit, for it was based upon strongly Christian principles; and then he identified it also with the religion of his childhood at home. " I saw that much of the life about me in the summer time was the application of the ideas and principles which formerly I had connected only with Sunday School, wearing one's best clothes, and stained glass. My enthusiasm for this summer home was then transformed into an enthusiasm for the Christian way of life, and as this became clearer to me, it raised the question of my own life-investment and the future. Could I be enthusiastic about the Christian way of life without its costing me something? Was this ' something ' more than I was prepared to give? Such a state of mind, with its vague enthusiasm and its dim uneasiness, became characteristic of my vacation life. I wish that I had known then what I know now, that God shows His will only *decision by decision*, day by day. One only gets the full picture as he strikes out on what he has and knows. God never lets us down—it's safe to trust those inner urgings,—safer than we know."

Then came college, and this is his comment upon his education: " School and college were never very kind to my spiritual self. In a very real way, they played a kind of Mr. Hyde to the camp's Dr. Jekyll. Not that there was anything obviously perverting in the high school building where I studied, or on the campus. Certainly my mind is a better organ in consequence of these years of preparation, and I am rich in friends made there; my disposition, naturally shy, improved, and life opened up wonderfully. Milestones were passed in quick succession, for life was great fun. The trouble lay in this rollicking campus life being entirely too easy. Never built for an athlete, I soon looked for other fields in which to win laurels. I gave my energy first to studies, and then in ever-increasing amounts to the well-known extracurricular activities,—dramatics, managing officerships, endless committees. Class-room work on the whole was not thrilling, but I found that time and pains bore fruit—and a pleasant pat on the back.

"There are many reasons why I am grateful to the university for the life which it gave me, and many reasons why I think of it as something inadequate and even dangerous. What I regret most about it was its failure to make me ask searching questions—questions such as invariably popped up at the camp in July and August. How about the future? What claims, if any, has religion upon one's life? What is 'doing one's best'? Should we be 'practical' or 'idealistic' in viewing the world? What about these reports of pain and suffering? (Notice the detachment of that word 'reports.') What was the significance of that strange little three-lettered word 'sin'? The winter brought its questions, but quite different ones,—much consulting with one's comrades, but little with one's own self or with God. The soil at college was rich, to be sure, but the wrong things seemed to be growing in it,—selfishness, self-satisfaction, and an absurdly sophisticated, hopelessly one-sided attitude towards one's own place in the sun."

I remember him very well in these days of his university life. He was one of the "big men" of the campus. He was secretary and treasurer of his class.

There were seven bank accounts of various college organizations for which he was responsible. He was a man to call on if you wanted something done. He was in the councils of the college mighty. You would see him wheeling about the campus in his busy but relaxed fashion, with always time for a genial word and a thoughtful remembrance, but he was usually on his way to a committee—the undergraduate schools, the class officers, or the senior council. Many an undergraduate today is as busy as a bank-president, with a morning full of classes, and an afternoon and evening full of appointments. The undergraduate is likely to be a premature man of the world, as the alumnus is likely to be (when back in the college town) an overgrown schoolboy. Men like this are receiving an excellent equipment for doing well in life's competition: but, of course, the deeper purpose of education is to provide such a sense of value in life as will create motive. He speaks of his " sense of power and importance. But there were dull moments and worse. More and more things had come into my life of which I was ashamed. Several times I was surprised at myself for allowing what had formerly been a temptation of the imagination to become very concrete sin. I met the situation by ever more and more activity. I answered the rising questions by trying to forget them. And I decided that spring of my Senior year definitely to go into business."

" Dickens has a character in Oliver Twist called the 'Artful Dodger.' Such an one was I for the five ensuing years during which I attempted to avoid a conscience, my own better judgment, and a ' still, small voice ' which with annoying persistence questioned my way of life. Buttressing this inner urge was the influence of four of my friends, who were at times most annoying. They followed my uneasy figure amid the granite and the rush of downtown New York, and then to the comfortable precincts of a dormitory in New England, where I lived during a strenuous session at law school, and lastly back into the town where I had gone to college. The voice of first one, then another, of these ' troublers of Israel,' kindly but challenging, kept reminding me that telephones and case-books and the murmur of a pleasantly efficient office-force were not adequate substitutes for the particular will of God for me—and by this time they knew that I was far from sure that any of these was or had been God's will in my life. We might talk of angels' wings and the fascinating abstractions of the Christian religion, but sooner or later we came back to the here and now and to just what each one of us was doing about the inescapable call of the Christ. ' Yes, but is that your *best*,' they would ask in their delightfully insinuating way: ' Is that what God really wants of you? '

" There was one peak. It was a Sunday afternoon in March, 1921. I had been in business for nine months, everything was outwardly flourishing. A few days before one of my incarnation-of-conscience friends had made a very practical suggestion: that I should take some time out, and listing in one column all my reasons for being in business, and then in another all my reasons for going into the ministry. On the afternoon in question I did this; I was surprised to have the scale tilt towards the ministry. I tried to change the score, and make it tilt the other way: but there was plenty of time to think that afternoon, and I could not get away from the truth. Then I prayed about it, and the ministry seemed all the clearer as I waited in an unhurried silence. I remember standing up all alone in my room and saying, with supreme happiness, ' Yes, I'll do it, I'll do it! ' That night I met one of my friends on the side of the angels, and told him about it, much to his surprise and joy."

But here fear and selfishness reclaimed him. He began to wonder and to debate. There were so many things at stake—so many lives to consider. He would wait and consult with the president, and so on, and so on. Now, there is no graver mistake that any man can make than to let God's clear will wait upon any human approval whatsoever. In the days of making up one's mind, it is advantageous to talk with a few people to whom God's will is real and who seek it first. But once the mind is made up, upon the best light one has, heeding the oft-repeated urges which nothing can repress, do not ask the Holy Spirit to stand at any man's doorstep and wait for his concurrence. Drummond's advice here is sound: "Never reconsider once the decision has finally been made." This man reconsidered; how he rued it let him say himself:

"Now and then when people talk enthusiastically about the value of a ' broad experience '—how splendid for Tom to study law before taking up teaching, or for Dick to sell bonds before going to medical school, or for Harry to try ' the world ' before he goes into the ministry, I want to choke them. No experience, however broad, is right if it is experience without God's will. Fortunately, He does make use of our mistakes and redeem gloriously what has been utterly lost. But—to play about as I did, with the thought that, after all, God's will was always there to come back to, and that meanwhile experience was experience, and therefore excellent, is playing with moral and spiritual fire. The worst of it is that you can't see the danger until the damage is done." What he means by this will emerge as the story proceeds.

He wavered in his decision, thought for a time he would stay in the business where he was; and then decided upon a kind of compromise. He would go into the law. This was not "money-grubbing," it was a "profession," and it took brains. The autumn found him at the law school, working at high pressure in one of the most difficult academic institutions in the world, drowning the call to the ministry in his desire to excel, in pride, in over-conscientiousness. With health never robust, and with a division in the inner citadel of the heart, here are the materials for a first-class tragedy. The stage was set for a break-down, and an attack of grippe the following spring began the play. Examinations must be foregone. Hopes cracked and broke. For six years he has carried with him the results of that wrong step in a weakened body. " The law school experience," he says, " was splendid experience. But at what a price! "

" Wrong decisions," he goes on, " are apt to bring other and more subtle consequences. That year's experience left my mind in a turmoil of dissatisfaction. Far from being now turned promptly to the ministry by these disheartening months, the inner conflict seemed all the more acute, and the future dark indeed. One part of me longed to re-enter the law school as soon as possible and reclaim what illness had snatched away from me: and this I eventually did. There is no need to say more than that it resulted in a still further reduction of physical strength."

Places are infectious, and it was a merciful good

sense which eventually turned his steps away from the place of his wrong choice and his failure, to the place of his early aspirations, the place which nourished the still repressed urge towards the ministry. He went back to the camp. "There," says he, "I began to hear again the same voices and began asking myself the old questions. One hot August morning the camp director found me writing letters on the counter of the camp-store, and said, 'You're preaching to us next Sunday.' I made some facetious reply, but looked up to see a very serious face peering into a Western Union telegram. 'Here you are, Mr. ——— can't come, and I want you to give the boys a talk in his place.' I told him that preaching a sermon was the last thing I could tackle. Inside I was a-flutter in a curious way: secretly I felt a great hope that he would insist. He did. I shoved my unanswered letters into a box, and walked down towards the shore to breathe fresh air and think. The camp had always brought to me a vision and a hope—it was only right for me to say a bit about that: and I thought about Saul on the Damascus Road and his vision. A vision was a rich experience which called for gratefulness in the beholder—and then, a decision. This, I knew, was good psychology and good religion. When a place or a situation or a personality or all three together touched the soul of a man, and pointed out things new and wonderful, that man ought to do something about it. Certainly. I sat down and began to write. 'Vision, decision, then courage to carry out the new hopes into action.' The talk fairly flowed. Illustrations came bounding into my mind.

"Next morning I spent the day on the spot where I had been admitted into the mysteries of Indian lore, and where I had seen Seton Thompson twirl a set of sticks before a gaping crowd of youngsters till a pile of wood shavings caught fire. With the manuscript in my hand, sitting on a pile of logs, I read it over.

"I had written that the major decisions of life must be made as a result of, and in line with, one's visions. As I went over this part again, I suddenly began to realize how effectively I was preaching,—that the real preaching had already begun and that the congregation was myself! I thought about initiation on that summer day years before into the interesting but infinitely unimportant Indian lore: was I initiated into the religion I was to talk to these boys about on Sunday? I thought of Seton Thompson setting those chips afire: was I yet set on fire of the Spirit? In those few intervening days till Sunday came, I went back often to the place to repeat the talk to the pine trees (very good homiletical experience, this, by the way) 'vision, decision, courage'—and each time came back the question, 'What about yourself? What about yourself?' Then Saturday afternoon came. I read over the end of the talk: 'So when you've seen your goal, when you've decided to seek it, then fight it out, unafraid . . . striving for the best, *only* for the best. In the words of Paul, 'But one thing I do: forgetting those things which are behind and reaching forward unto the things which are before, I press on towards the goal.' That ended the talk. I repeated the words slowly.

"'That ends not the talk only, but the whole business, the whole business,' I said to myself. 'Someone else speaks at chapel tomorrow, unless . . . unless.' One can't look out at two hundred and fifty boys, and a group of his own friends, who know him and love him, and talk about decisions like these, unless he has made the decision himself. So I could not say what I had written: it was impossible, absolutely impossible, unless . . . There I saw the figure of cross-roads: here was I pointing others to one road while I went in another direction myself. It was late, but not yet too late. With that my heart gave a bound, and for a moment everything around me, birds, leaves, wood-sounds, seemed to cease, as though Someone were waiting expectantly. I looked up again into the blue sky, and the innermost recesses of my being felt alive in a new, alarming, delightful way. My lips opened, and I spoke, and the words were words of freedom and of joy, ' O God, if Thou canst use me now, at last I am ready.' There was a sudden, indescribable light-ness of body and mind; and the joy with which I *then* spoke out the talk, and the joy with which I fairly shouted it next morning above the rustlings of the woods about our out-of-door chapel, is a joy which simply defies all powers of description or imagination. A few days later I told some of my friends that I had decided to study for the ministry."

The autumn found him in a theological seminary where, he says, " a whole host of vague doubts about clergymen and the Church dissolved like a mist before the sun. My enthusiasm for the ministry multiplied a hundredfold. A course on the Life of Christ made the most fascinating Personality in history a living reality to me, and I began to learn how little I had actually known of Jesus. There was sound intellectual stimu-lus, and time for prayer such as I had never had before." I remember a letter which he wrote to me during this time in which he said, " I am almost too enthusiastic about everything here. Bless you for making me be my best self! Nothing else is worth while for long. Now it is merely a case of *having* to do what I *want* to do." For the first time the conflict was resolved, the rift in his conscience was healed, the two sides of his life came together; and he was at one with himself when he gave himself to the doing of God's will.

During that year there had begun for him a steady practice of an early morning Quiet Time: this resulted from his having been struck with the twelfth verse of the sixth chapter of St. Luke. During one of those periods of unhurried waiting upon God, the leading came that he should make a great venture across the sea to continue his preparation in Scotland. There has never been overmuch money in the family, and there were other objections as well: but the following autumn saw him in Edinburgh, these obstacles having faded out of the picture, and his original guidance having proved its own validity. The intellectual and spiritual fires of Edinburgh never go out, and all Presbyterian parsons would like to study there at some point in their career. Here was continued the mental discipline which had been begun in America, and he says, " I learned a new reverence and humbleness. Scottish frankness, self-reliance, simplicity and earnestness stimulated me: and there was an abundance of kindness, too."

The college where he studied closed its term that year in March, and after a period of rest, Sufficient Grace set off to visit Durham, Lincoln, York and London. " In due course," he goes on, " I alighted at the G. W. R. station at Oxford. In a curious but definite way I had been fairly propelled towards Oxford by a series of circumstances, and I felt a sense of rightness as I stepped into the town earlier than I had expected, with three days still remaining before the opening of the Oxford term. In Oxford, at the time, were several of my old friends who had become enthusiastic members of the First Century Christian Fellowship. They were enrolled in various colleges, and I hoped to look them up, but only as sightseeing permitted. I had a fear that a 'house-party' might be in the offing, and I was still afraid of 'house-parties.' My religious experience thus far, though it had been influenced by many people, was curiously solitary; and I felt no eagerness to be drawn into a religious affair which was avowedly social. The morning after my arrival, however, a great square-shouldered Scotsman who burst upon me out of nowhere, and, as I feared, offered me an invitation to a house-party which was 'just beginning this afternoon!' After one refusal, which was good-naturedly not accepted, I found myself being whisked along a hedge-lined road, in the car of an American friend, towards a village called Wallingford. Seated next me, and trying to remember to drive on the left, this friend told me of his last eight months in America and his first three in England, the story of modern apostolic Christianity working with pagan youth. It was a thrilling tale: there was criticism, misunderstanding, and a deep, daily dependence upon God. I felt I was back in New Testament days, when some were changed and some were scandalized. I was impressed. I liked his childlike attitude of trust in God, and I admired his courage. And I thought: 'Something here for me.'

"I don't know exactly what I expected to find at Wallingford. At that time a great many idle tales were being circulated about house-parties by persons who had never spent a day at one of them. My own head sheltered a lot of weird ideas. The first thing I actually saw, as the car drove up an avenue of pines and stopped at the entrance to the inn, was a couple of remarkably good tennis players having a go on a grass-court. My Scotsman appeared in white flannels. By supper I had met six or eight English undergraduates, and some Americans—all of them delightful. There was nothing of the stuffy prayer-meeting about it. The house-party lasted three days, and each was better than the last. There were group meetings and Quiet Times kept unitedly and time for long talks with people. Nothing was forced or hurried or ' scheduled ' in the way of ordinary conferences. What was said was simple, interesting and helpful.

" It began to make a change in my conception of the ministry. Here were students, not the kind one would expect to find at a religious gathering, who were being brought to a new and abiding consciousness of God's presence and His claims upon their lives. I had long known theoretically that this was what I wanted to do in my own ministry, and now I saw how wholly inadequate was my own little isolated programme. The power and discipline of the group were new to me: I both admired and feared them. Yet here were spiritual results which I was not having in my own life. I saw that a ' lone-wolf ' conception of working for Christ was ridiculous and wrong. I saw that there was an ocean of pride between myself and this Fellowship where each shared in a common task, and no one got the credit: this pride in myself had to be faced frankly. I saw that I had never really entrusted my *time* to God—that, always afraid of slighting my studies, or doing poorly in them, I had been rigid and

selfish about the way I had budgeted the working day.
There had been real lack of trust in God here, and not
enough confidence that if He wanted me to have it,
He would guide me about my intellectual preparation. I had been as tight with my time as some of
my acquaintances whom I had criticized had been
with their money. I began to change my attitude
towards prayer: for some years I had been praying
and seeking God's guidance about questions which
humanly I considered important. Now I saw how
foolish it was to interpose my own wisdom concerning what was important, and how dangerous is such
a division in the mind when one comes to prayer.
Any number of new questions popped up which I had
never considered topics for prayer; and I realized for
the first time that the Lord *might* be interested in the
hour I arose on Monday morning, as well as in what
seminary I attended, or what church I might preach in
later on.

" The last night of the house-party I spoke for perhaps ten minutes, mentioning some of the new convictions which had come to me, and some of the obstacles
in me which with God's help I wanted to change.
Those words marked a new advance for me spiritually.
They brought me in from spiritual isolation to a
shoulder-to-shoulder fellowship and a bond with these
men and women who were there which has been the
greatest single factor for good in these last years of my
life. Before that few days' visit in Oxford was over,
it had lengthened into nine weeks; during those nine
weeks I learned that the experience of Christ and His
Gospel, while it is an intensely individual affair in
certain of its aspects, is always one-sided without the
corrective and expansion which comes from intimate

association with those farther along the trail than one-self. The sort of fellowship which I found in this group is rare: I have not seen so searching and un-compromising, nor yet so gay and merry, a fellowship anywhere else. At my next house-party I had the joy of carrying one person through a surrender into a new personal fellowship with God. At another I learned still more about the pain which is involved in merging one's life into a spiritual fellowship, of thoroughly working with a group, sharing with them, being ' checked ' by them when it was necessary, and at times having to obey one's spiritual teacher. Protestantism has lost the note of spiritual authority, and it will never return through mere spiritual officialism: but it may come back through a fellowship which knows no human authority save that which deserves to be recognized through its own manifest spiritual advancement and effectiveness.

"About a year and a half ago I was ordained. Just before that my health had taken a turn for the worse, and since that time I have had strength to preach just once! There has not been much pain, but often days and days of weakness, feeling good for absolutely nothing, and stretches of lethargy from fever. Suffer-ing no longer frightens me: it is here, and I've learned to try not to escape it, but after science has done its best, to accept it, and then look to God for strength and then for its significance. I remember one occasion when I had had three successive set-backs, I turned to God in utter despair: and the answer was that I felt Him actually at work within me in a positive and physical way, and there came with it a new lease of spiritual life and hope. God uses suffering when we let Him: once I was taken ill at a house-party, and instead of dashing home I was guided to remain; people came to my room as I was able to see them, and some vital interviews took place. I also got well before the party was over, and so shook off my fear of being ill in a crowded environment. Sometimes I have been able to use my illness to help people who could not have been reached unless someone had a message on suffering and trouble. Last winter I had the ' flu ' twice, and began to feel very sorry for myself indeed, and to question God's power to use me at all: shortly afterwards, the conviction came that it was nothing but a sin to put oneself on the shelf, and that the Lord could always work where there was a willingness to serve. In a new attitude I looked around me, and almost at once three contacts were used to bring a young business man into the group, a fellow whom I had missed completely when I had been well and active.

" Complete trust about the future *is* a task. I hate uncertainty and not knowing what I can and ought to do. When fear comes in, I ' stew ' and faith ceases. In the train of that kind of fear, all the old problems of temptation come back. The selfward look is fatal: only the Godward look is full of hope. I am learning that following Christ means taking life day by day, finding strength for the task at hand, and trusting the rest of it—all of it. Only recently have they discovered the underlying cause of my illness: it has cost a great deal of time and money, and promises to cost a great deal more. I have had to change completely my programme of life, postpone what I eagerly want to do, and for long periods mark time without sufficient strength to do any work at all. The illness may be incurable, and whatever success is achieved in the direction of a cure, my body will never be robust. It was my own wilfulness and disobedience which has weakened and shortened my life. Yet some of the deepest lessons I have learned, of patience, of trust, of the willingness to fail, have come through the surrender of the consequences of my wrong choice to God. Perhaps one day I shall be well enough to take a church, and if so, all right: if not, why still, all right! God can and will support me. He knows where I can be trusted, and where I am still unfaithful. To Him belongs the plan and its fulfilment. If illness comes, I can through it seek ways to grow;—a special kind of growth. Only no kicking! So long as the barriers of sin—rebellion, self-pity, the sins which fester in idleness—are faced and destroyed through confession, prayer and forgiveness, spiritual growth need never stop. Whatever happens to the body, our souls can live and live indeed, come what may. This is the life that makes us free."

And we remember another strong, afflicted life in the long ago, who in spite of a defective frame swerved the course of human history, and who tells us of himself in these words:

" There was given to me a thorn in the flesh, the messenger of Satan to buffet me, lest I should be exalted above measure. For this thing I besought the Lord thrice, that it might depart from me. And he said unto me, My grace is sufficient for thee: for my strength is made perfect in weakness. Most gladly therefore will I rather glory in my infirmities, that the power of Christ may rest upon me." *

* II Corinthians 12:7-9.

IX

THE MILITANT MYSTIC

ONE of the quarrels which our practical Western world has with mysticism is that we associate it with supine and incompetent people. We think of it as a dissipator of energy, instead of as a source of it. We think of certain unfortunate oriental examples of it, and picture it as idle, draining away power which ought to have been invested in human concerns. But the true mystics find in their communion with the Unseen precisely the fountain of that sustained and enthusiastic idealism which is of so much creative value in human society. Real mysticism bestows a quality of inner energy which is often patent to the most casual observer. It is so evident in the subject of this sketch.

He was born with native physical energy. He sometimes walks across a floor as if he would stave it in with his heel. He goes down a street as if mighty business awaited him at his destination. There is a radiant force which is always given off by a healthy, powerful, tingling, disciplined body: and the air of almost any room is charged with extra electricity the moment this man comes into it. I saw him once hold the best wrestler in college longer than was flattering to the latter's vanity, though the Mystic makes no professional pretensions at wrestling. All this might have remained mere animal spirits had not an exquisite sympathy redeemed it and spiritualized it; had not the lamb lain down with the lion. As it is, he can come into a sick-room, and impart to an ill person a kind of divine jealousy of being well and exhale a health which they seem to appropriate to themselves by a process which I think no psychologist can quite chart.

The first thing you notice about him is his eyes. They will snap at you with challenge, they will leap with imagination or sheer well-being, they will wink at you with understanding, they will flash with zeal, and, on occasion with indignation, and then twinkle with mischief and merriment. He is almost a genius at enunciating " principle," as we call the basic assumptions of this whole message: and one often sees him go in half a minute from some law-and-prophets deliverance, to an amused laughter at himself for his own solemnities. Surely here is a healthy and happy alternation for a soldier of the Lord!

He tells me that in his childhood there were three outstanding influences. His father has always been vivid, capable, ambitious; yet scrupulous till one thinks he must have been heir to the conscience of John Calvin himself.

" From mother," he says, " I inherited a mystical quality which believed implicitly in God and instinctively in His capacity to guide. With this there went a desire for practical helpfulness in relating people together, for I saw my mother living as a sort of useful clearing-house, knowing always those in the community who needed help, and having an uncanny way of knowing just who could help them. Early reverses in the family made me care more for money than I should have, and gave me some fears about not having enough: but this never cramped the feeling of being able, whether rich or poor, to serve one's fellow-men."

The third great influence was " a rich memory of Presbyterianism in the person of the minister of our church, a distant cousin for whom I happened to be named. He had a theology which was conservative, but not contentious, which believed in miracles, and which issued in visible fruits of the Spirit."

Adolescence had brought a sharp conflict with this energetic father, and the confidence of the boy was later withdrawn from him altogether and its place was taken by an argumentative and combative attitude on his part which made the time at college and during the war period, which broke during his university course, " a very lonely path." The fledglings must get out of the nest and fly with their own wings: but is there anything more needed today than something which can make that separation between parents and adolescents less abrupt and bitter than it often is? As one sees the message told about in this book, spreading into families whose little children are included in its discovery, one of the deepest hopes of all is that adolescence, with all its strains and tensions, may find parents and children already so closely welded together that when the parents are needed most, they can serve most. In this work, we are already happily beginning to see that this will be the result.

His loneliness engendered in him " a dry human conscientiousness to earn my own way, to be financially independent, to satisfy a craving for achievement for its own sake by the power of my own will, and so I began shaping my life around this idea. Schopenhauer, Nietzsche, Whitman, had their successive fascinations. Yet somewhere deeper still I believed in the Christian religion. The one thing I could not do was to make its power work in my own life. I could not conquer inner defeat, nor combat my sense of loneliness about life, with its apparent need for inexorable human competition. It bred a fear about the future and a desire for some form of outward security, such as financial independence, social status, or recognized achievement. Beneath all of these was an undercurrent of wonderment: ' why live at all? ' "

I remember this spindling youth in his early college days, on his way towards a Phi Beta Kappa key, busy about college, sound in mind and body, grinning most of the time: and none would have suspected in him any such dark thoughts as " why live at all? "

Then came the war with its jarring and testing of the fundamental ends of life, and he returned from the service at the end of what would have been his Junior year, pretty much disillusioned.

He had taken all along a casual interest in the work of the Christian Association at college. He thought of it as an institution, useful principally because of some of its activities, such as teaching English to Italians, and running a boys' camp. Some of us had seen that organization slide down from being at one time a great spiritual force into being a highly-organized piece of social service: and we were eager to bring it back to its original purpose and make it a religious power on the campus. This wanted a few men who had themselves had a genuine religious experience. Accordingly, we invited forty or fifty undergraduates to meet with us in conference before the beginning of the Mystic's Senior year. We did not talk about organizations or committees or budgets: we talked about what some of our

own needs had been and what Christ had done and
was doing for us.

"Four people made an impression upon me that
week-end," he says. "The first man's honest sharing
of his own need and of the way Christ had helped him,
gave me for the first time confidence in ultimate victory over inner defeat. The second told a story of
surrender to Christ which punctured my pride and
ambition. The third got across to me the power of
disciplined and Christ-inspired love for one's fellow-
men. The challenge of the fourth lay in a sheer life
of guidance and faith. But," he adds, "the week-end
proved to be a distinct jolt, for I was not prepared for
the critical self-examination which it called for. My
first impulse was to protect myself by means of revolt,
and I proceeded to search out two kindred spirits,
under similar conviction, and do so. We held indignation meetings by ourselves, we infected the atmosphere with criticism. As I think back on it, I know
that I was convinced in spite of myself that you all
had the answer to my problem, and by a curious con-
tradiction in my own mind, I found myself searching
you out absolutely against my will, disliking the very
thought of it and yet wanting to tell you all about
myself."

Not until after he returned to college did he make
any fundamental decision for Christ. Some of us were
meeting daily for the enrichment of our spiritual experience, in a well-remembered upper room. The
most pressing problem in his life was his relation to his
father: and one day I there held up to him what was
practically involved in confession and restoration to his
father for the wrong in his antagonism of five years'
standing. We faced then the other issues involved in

his complete commitment to Christ. And then he made it, alone and by himself. He declares that "That year with its constant outpouring of generous fellowship convinced me most deeply of the quality of life that could be one's possession if the conditions were fulfilled. I have never tried to deceive myself or convince myself, even when I was not living it in my own life, that this was not the highest vision for human existence than I have ever seen."

Now here are two strains battling in a man's life for the mastery. He has not had wealth, but he knows that he has the ability to get it. An invisible but very real gallery looks down upon the struggle in this arena of a man's life-warfare, a gallery vaguely called "the world," which always claps at success and turns down its thumbs at failure. And then there is another gallery, represented by a much smaller company; and in their midst a grave Figure is also looking down, and in His eyes is written a great expectation. A man's life is hanging in the balance: shall he choose an immediate success, which may prove to be in the long run a failure, or shall he follow where those grave Eyes seem to be looking, across a possible immediate failure, to an ultimate achievement? Every man must wage a battle in that arena, with those spectators. And the way he chooses carves a destiny for time and eternity.

For a time our friend took the way of immediate success. He had been offered a promising position with one of the growing investment companies of New York, and he took it. He threw himself into it with the desperate enthusiasm of the man who is not sure that he is where he ought to be.

One day, as he was travelling, he picked up Philip Cabot's article in *The Atlantic Monthly,* of August,

1923, called "The Conversion of a Sinner." "I first saw the fruit of self-will in this man's break-down," he says. "It revealed me to myself as really living independently of Christ's power and direction, really leaning on my own strength for every important decision. There was something in it which broke down the walls of my resistance, and I found myself speeding along on a train out of Pittsburgh, thinking entirely new thoughts and feeling entirely new values. I thought about giving up business, of the surprise and ridicule of my friends at resigning from so rewarding a position. I thought of the ministry and of the kind of life which the Fellowship called for. That night I decided to 'launch out into the deep:' and with the decision to cast my will and my life on God, there came an indescribable sense of relief, of burdens dropping away."

The work together that following winter manifested to him, as he says, "the infinite pains which are necessary to forge a working spiritual fellowship out of a collection of individual decisions for Christ. It showed me clearly the difference between belief in institutionalism and ultimate belief in personality. The conviction grew that year that one must put one's deepest faith in people, in God-directed, Christ-filled personality, and in the promises of Christ Himself. The corollary to this is that the great necessity for Christian work today is the forging of an unbreakable human fellowship under God."

In these days of domestic instability, perhaps the most difficult and strategic place to begin such work is in one's own home. We must now say something of the possibilities of married life upon a basis of complete surrender on both sides to God's will and His steady guidance. In this instance, his wife was not wholly in accord with him at the time of their marriage. She had been for years cultivating an exquisite voice, and preparing for its public use, so soon as she should have completed her training. It is difficult sometimes to separate artistic concentration from selfishness; and now her life's dream must either be modified, or his work must be given up, or else they must go their separate ways, using their home only as a kind of railway station for two, where their tracks should meet occasionally. Here is material for a broken engagement, or for an unhappy marriage. An armed truce is often the true inwardness of what passes for marriage. With infinite patience, the Militant Mystic set about to win the one who was closest to him in the world, who watched him day by day, saw his every slip and was the loving but surest critic. By faith in her, by tact, by honesty, by love that dared expect the very highest, she was won to a complete commitment of her life to Jesus Christ and His will for her and for the two together. There began a deeper intimacy, a truer love than any they had known before. She gave up the career, merged her life into the double vision, uses her voice constantly for the joy of her friends and as a service to Christ, but her call is not to the concert stage, it is to the winning of women for Christ. Professor Hocking has a sentence in one of his great books * which seems to me to catch in a few words the genius of Christian marriage: " The only being you can love is the being who has an independent object of worship, and that holds you out of your self-indulgence to a worship of that same object." Is it not this *Tertium Quid* which is the absent element

* *Human Nature and Its Remaking*, p. 363.

in many failing marriages, this relation to God, for the Christian, which makes true marriage, not a straight line between two persons, but rather a triangle which includes a Third? To very few men is given grace to win their wives to full commitment to Christ after marriage. But this relationship was guided, and the Militant Mystic speaks thankfully of " the one person who bore the brunt of the work cheerfully, without in any way complaining, and whose full acceptance of the demands of a life of faith in Christ, and whose adaptability of home and desires and dreams and talents towards that one end was a constant source of strength. There are few people that I know who have as fully assumed the cost of this quality of life in marriage as she." Any man can say pleasant things about his wife: but these two I know deeply, and I know what a monument to their patient faith is their present exquisitely unpossessive relationship, so freely sharing one another with all who are in need, and so effective as they are in bringing to other lives the abundant life which they found in Christ.

To return to the idea expressed before, " The great necessity for Christian work today is the forging of an unbreakable human fellowship under God." The accomplishment of this began when he later succeeded to the leadership of the Christian Association, where he gathered about him an exceptional group of workers.

A second worker was a man who had come to a near-by theological seminary in the fall after his graduation from one of the most socially advantageous of the smaller colleges of the East. In college he had been popular, a good athlete, no star as a scholar (he says, " I took a four-year course in five years "), but attractive and lovable and very good-looking. A man I know who was a class or two behind him used to idolize him and envy him from a distance, as doubtless did many of his juniors. It was largely his family's religion which was carrying him into the ministry, and an attempt to measure up to what they thought of him. There is a very subtle temptation which besets a man like this when he gets to a seminary: being obviously of more distinction than most of his colleagues, he chooses for his friends the more attractive, and does not delay to emphasize certain of his own more worldly connections. This man did not wear ministerial clothes, he ran with an interesting crowd; he set himself apart socially from the other men, and he had a gift for smoking a pipe as though he were doing it a favour. Having gone to one or two house-parties while he was an undergraduate, he knew the Militant Mystic, and was soon a guest in the tower-room where his office was. Here they talked, uncovered the unsuspected inferiorities for which social success was a compensation, got at basic motives, and the theological student made a surrender of his life to Christ. The development of this man from a rather callow youth into a sensitive and intelligent worker for Christ, able to win the confidence of men many years his senior and carry them into further reaches of Christian experience, has been primarily the work of the Militant Mystic.

A third worker was a scholarly lad, who had the reputation of being able to think in Latin, but who in his early days certainly did not think in terms of human beings. Had he gone into the ministry as he was, he would have been another of the many scholars who are divorced from life, who know books but not men, and therefore in whose learning and teaching there is something forever incurably academic. Under his very eyes he had seen a room-mate changed from an indolent and uninteresting fellow to a real force for Christ: this made him ask himself questions about his own religion; why could he not have helped this man in such a way? In a spirit of mild curiosity about an interesting spiritual phenomenon, he came around. The Militant Mystic had something. It interested him. He kept coming. He came down out of his scholarly clouds and began to work with actual people. Scholarship became a means, not an end. He became the closest associate of the Mystic in his work, and for years has seconded him with amazing courage, understanding and loyalty.

In these years the lives of these last two men have become more and more closely interwoven into that of the Militant Mystic. They form two links in the unbreakable chain. The relationship between the three is paradoxical enough, the same paradox always present when men try to apply a perfect belief to an imperfect world. From the outside one sees the younger man learning to subordinate personal inclinations with the desire to second the older as effectively and as unobtrusively as possible, their eyes to the largest service of the three instead of to the largest personal reward. They know how to play second and do it well. Yet in their own minds there is no such rôle as second. The only work to do is God's will. That is always primary, all-important. There is real belief that through the power of God each man can be made perfect, complete, able to do all things. They are content to let God show the way for the broadening growth of each one. They have learned a much-needed lesson in this individualistic age that if men aim at unity, they find the diversity of gifts; if they aim at diversity, they find chaos.

Guidance has carried the Militant Mystic into the thick of the work as it opened up in some of the English and Scottish universities, and again in Holland. Two years ago he brought back with him, for a great house-party, an Oxford Rhodes scholar from South Africa, who has since become the entering-wedge for the work in his native land; and a Welsh "hearty" from Oxford, who had been profoundly touched through the work of the movement in England. The Militant Mystic is at his best in the direction of a team of travelling workers, disciplining them, carrying them further stretches in their own experience, teaching them to make a natural and fruitful approach to others. The patience and insight which this requires cannot be exaggerated. And it goes so much deeper into the roots of the men themselves than does ordinary religious training, that the men reach early in their careers a kind of maturity, a trust in God, an expectancy in any given situation, which often outstrips their seniors in such work.

This kind of work has in recent years strengthened and extended the bonds in the living fellowship about the Militant Mystic. One summer's work reclaimed a young man of good family who for ten years following the war had been a vagabond with drink and prize-fighting his chief diversions. The story of how he was reached at a house-party, of his conversion, and how subsequently he decided to enter the Christian ministry is told in " From a Far Country."

Without his own home, without a regular income, without a " position " in the ordinary sense, living on faith, going where he is led, giving himself lavishly to a few people at a time, forging leaders out of them as soon as they are able, the Militant Mystic lives actually more like an apostle, and conducts his work more nearly upon apostolic lines, than any man I know, except Frank Buchman. For many lives, of which I cheerfully acknowledge myself to be one, he holds an unique challenge. With extraordinary love, he can yet be extraordinarily honest: and he detects spiritual second-best with deadly certainty. Across the grave of young William Borden, in Cairo, is written, "Apart from Christ there is no explanation of such a life." It might be written across this man's life, too.

X

HOPEFUL

MOST of us would say that pragmatism, taken literally, would not hold water: because a thing " works " is no guarantee that it corresponds with reality and is necessarily true. But there is a kind of negative pragmatism which *is* true: namely, that what will *not* work is *not* true. The majority of us have a sufficiently instinctive loyalty to life to discard that which ultimately and in the long run makes it harder and less worthwhile. Our quarrel with materialism and behaviourism and humanism is not so much a theoretical quarrel, but comes from the fact that these ways of looking at life have not lifted our views of it, but lowered them; not opened to us further sources of energy for living life fully, but cut us off from them and thrown us back still further upon our own meagre powers. We feel that philosophy has no more business running life down than religion has in sentimentalizing it. Here the thing is—and we have got to get on with it as best we can. We believe that these cold-water theories will be routed in the end of the day, not for any abstract or rational reason whatever, but because their contractile views of life and human nature have made our existence more intolerable and not less: they have already lost our confidence by what we have seen of their fruits, when as yet our minds have not learned to defeat them by argument.

In the meantime they have spread a miasma of misgiving. It is now fashionable to think ill of human nature, to be contemptuous of it, to deride as old-fashioned those who take an optimistic view of it. The common view today is that human beings are bundles of instincts wrapped in a body: the world is a cage, and man is an animal inside it. Gild the cage, plant flowers in it if you can, get what liberty when and how you may inside it, for these will make your captivity more bearable: but you are basically a beast, and when you die you will die like a dog. One agrees with these pessimists as to the miserable state of things at present: we would remind them that the prophets felt so of old. But we part company with them when it comes to possibilities. For so much evil is created by want of the faith that it need not be. And so much positive good is created by the presence of strong and hopeful and believing spirits. While these sad harbingers are croaking fatality on all sides, there are a little company of believers here and there who are actually keeping human nature from being futile. They are such people as would say with Hopeful, in *Pilgrim's Progress*, " Let us consider again, that all the law is not in the hand of Giant Despair. Others, so far as I can understand, have been taken by him as well as we; and yet have escaped out of his hand. Who knows, but that God that made the world, may cause that Giant Despair may die; or that at some time or other he may forget to lock us in; or but he may in a short time have another of his fits before us, and may lose the use of his limbs; and if ever that should come to pass again, for my part I am resolved to pluck up the heart of a man, and try my utmost to get from under his hand."

Here is the story of a modern Hopeful who has " resolved to pluck up the heart of a man," and not only try his utmost " to get from under his hand," but carry many another captive along with him.

He began with an average bringing up in a minister's family. His father was his chum. He liked the people and the church and the music. He had no inhibitions about being a minister's son, because his father was a happy, out-going, much-beloved man, and the lad was proud to be his son.

There was no adequate school in the town where they lived, so at ten he went off to a church boarding-school. " There I tumbled into the rough and hardy ways of boys who scrimmaged on the city pavements, played all manner of mean tricks, and looked angelic in their choir-stalls, for this was a choir school. It was a home-sick year. Gradually I learned to fight, hold my own with the other boys, not be bullied because I was a ' new kid,' and make friends. Music was never my long suit, so I spent more time alone than the other boys, time for mischief, and time for a boy's spurts at thinking, too." Later he went to another school in the country, where he rejoiced in the bliss of open fields, games, swimming, gathering birds' eggs and raiding apple-orchards in the autumn. There the religious instruction came from the mother of the head-master. " We giggled and were outrageously unmanageable," he confesses, " but we knew in our hearts that she loved Christ, and I can remember my indignation when the other boys would not listen and I wanted to. There were the regulation morning and evening prayers, but that was all the religion we had."

Picture an elderly lady, and two formal services a

day, as the entire spiritual stimuli for a pack of boys! It seems never to have occurred to the average schoolmaster that at the time when a lad is just beginning to be creative in every other way, he needs to be helped to be creative in religion. Most schools are glad to recognize signs of originality in athletics, art, manual training, literature: but all the while the drone of the daily chapel services is hummed out by someone else, the form of spiritual outlet is tame till it is tepid, and the Sacred Studies are usually stupid to the point of weariness. In few schools is there a man who knows how to win a boy's confidence and meet his deepest needs. The usual advisor at this juncture is a master who asks a boy into his room after lights, scares him half to death by looking very serious, and in an atmosphere charged with fear, begins what he calls a " frank talk together ": it is, of course, one-sided, the terrified lad agrees to everything in general, but feels no inclination to spread out his mind, open his problems, and seek further companionship with his advisor.

What is wanted is a man who naturally wins a boy's confidence, lets him talk when one day the right occasion offers, reaches a common level with him where discipline and disparity are utterly forgotten, gets the problems into the light, and helps the lad really to find an experience of Jesus Christ which will meet his problems. Then when two or three of these lads have begun their own private, daily Quiet Time, of prayer, Bible study, and listening for God's guidance, let them be brought into touch with one another, and a small group formed where they may thrash these matters out together, and into which slowly as other boys are truly touched, by the master or by themselves, they are brought for further fellowship and stimulus. Boys take to this message like ducks to water. The greatest stumbling-block to the formation of such a vital group as I have talked about lies in the want of a guiding hand, master or minister, who has a developed experience of Christ, but who also understands how to carry a boy over the difficult places in a growing religious experience. Hear the testimony of Hopeful as to the gaps in his own school religion:

" Hard grinding football practise and constant healthy outdoor living never took the place of an earnest, religious, wholesome, hygienic talk which I needed. I wanted to stand for the right things in school, and as far as possible I did. All that was needed was a deep and searching talk that would let the living Christ possess all the areas of my life for victorious living, and help me win that ceaseless battle with temptation and with the bitterness and distrust toward some of my companions which grew out of the rivalries of school elections." When I think of the dozens of boys whom he has helped with just such an " earnest, religious, wholesome, hygienic talk," it seems cruel that he could not have had it himself, just when he needed it most.

He went to a church college for a time, but during the War took a year out and taught in another church-school. He says that he found in force in this school the same custom of morning and evening chapel, with two services on Sunday. But here, with all the brightness of a happy school, and the sense of luxury and the very best of care, there still lurked in his soul the constant feeling that this religion was not related to the boys' interests and made an intimate reality in their daily living any more than it had been in his own school. But at that time his religion was more a matter of aspiration than of possession, and he had nothing to give.

He finished up his college career when the War was over, and fell from the standards which his home training had given him. He played bridge for a stake, finding it " a convenient way to supply himself with pocket-money." He drank, " not especially to get drunk but because I liked liquor, and if appetite got the better of caution, I did not mind." Life was very gay for him.

Then his father died, and there was a vast emptiness in this boy's heart.

" I hoped I could make my life count for righteousness as his had done," he told me. " If God wanted me in the ministry, I was willing to go, but I hoped not, for I had no developed convictions about the Christian message. Many times during the year after my father's death I was thrown with ministers, and I hoped to find in them a reality of Christian experience which would help me to integrate faith in Christ with the knowledge of the universe in which we live. I *thought* that my deepest needs were for a rational presentation of the Christian life, and helpful suggestions as to how one might really serve in the ministry along strictly humanitarian lines. I remember one learned minister with whom I spoke said, ' What you need to read is Thomas à Kempis and Thomas Aquinas.' I went to see the dean of a seminary, saying to him that I did not believe in the Virgin Birth. He asked me if I had read the New Testament recently, and when I said that I had not, he told me that I had better know more about it before I began to discuss theological points; and added, ' Is that all? ' He had cleared the ground for a good talk with me by showing me that I was intellectually half-baked; and then let me slip right through his fingers without ever getting where I lived. Back of my question about the Virgin Birth lay a searching, dissatisfied spirit. I think I wanted him to get at me personally, and tell me how I could carry on for Christ effectively in college. There were many inconsequential and inconclusive interviews like this.

"Then I went, one summer, to a conference on the ministry. I was the only one of the leaders of discussion groups for school-boys who had not himself decided to go into the ministry. We had three hundred promising boys. Great speakers, bishops and leaders, spoke to them in the morning meetings. I thought I would use the afternoons to get to know my group. I was surprised to find that most of the leaders were content to play tennis, or swim in the afternoon, and thought the morning meetings were enough. One night one of the younger leaders, who belonged to the First Century Christian Fellowship, got up in leaders' meeting and said, 'We are not challenging these boys to seek God's will for their lives. We are simply urging them to go into the ministry, without any reference to God's plan for the individual life. We are not helping them to itemize surrender to the will of God in their own lives, by getting down to their present needs: we are only talking about sin in the abstract. We are not helping them to see that the chief business of the ministry is to be fishers of men, and communicating to others the experience of the Radiant Christ.' He then went on to illustrate what he meant by telling us some stories of interviews which he had had the two days past, what needs he had found, and how an actual decision for Christ gave these boys new hope and a new grip on religion. To me this was all thrilling. I said to myself that this was what I was looking for, and I wanted to talk to him myself. As a matter of fact, he was so busy with seeing boys at that conference, all day long, that I never had a chance to talk to him. But later in the summer another man told me how this enthusiast about personal religion had helped him to see the joy of winning others to Christ."

By this time he had decided for the ministry himself and was going to seminary. He was not far from a large university, where several of the boys who had been at the conference on the ministry were Freshmen. He continued to keep in touch with them, and through them met a lot of others in the university. That winter he got into contact with a Freshman who was in great need. The following summer they went together to a student conference. He knew that they would find there the man who had so much impressed him the year before. He brought the two together, asking this member of the First Century Christian Fellowship if he would have a talk with the Freshman. The lad came back from the talk with his face shining, and immediately I went round to ask the older man how the talk had gone.

"How long have you known that boy?" he asked me.

"For about three or four months," I said.

"How often have you seen him during that time?" he queried.

"Several times a week, for long talks," I answered.

"Well, it's about time you quit asking other people to do your work," he said to me with a wink.

"That put a period to one part of my life and began

a new sentence. I knew I could not give what I did not have. I had to put up, or shut up. I knew that I needed to face a complete and unreserved surrender in my own life, and I did it after being perfectly honest with that man about my own inner life as I knew God saw me. Not long after, I was back at seminary where I met two old college friends. I forgot my surrender, and I stood them a couple of drinks, as I had done in the old days. Next morning in my Quiet Time came an uneasy sense of conviction that ought to have had something better for them than a drink. I knew that I had to go to those men and tell them of my surrender, and confess the lapse. I did so. I had only a few moments with one of them, and his chief reaction seemed to be amazement at my going a long distance to see him. He said nothing. Next day I got a letter from him, saying he wanted to live a Christian life, and was starting out. All through the summer came letters from him, telling of men he was getting in touch with, and of the abundant life he was finding in the service of the King. He writes:

" Conversion may be the work of a moment, but the implications of it are the work of a lifetime. The Fellowship realizes this truth, and helps in every way to see that surrender only begins a long warfare. There is need for daily surrender.

" The fellowship of a group who are seeking to express in their own lives the reality of Christ is almost indispensable to one who wants to grow. Here is where house-parties come in, with the chance to live together over a period of time, and learn from one another, and meet with those of different background, growth and experience. I have been a long time learning the difficult art of sharing this rich life with others. But my greatest desire has been to live convincingly for Christ, and to have the grace, the humility, the courage to witness for Him."

Hopeful is always after the "bad boy." He gets hold of them when they come out of prison, he finds them when they are drunk. He is not so much older, or more formal, but that they quickly feel he understands them. The narration of a prank of his own breaks the ice. One of them stole cars, and Hopeful made Christ real to him so that he became honest. He always has a yarn about one of these problem youngsters: he is an informal big-brother to dozens of them.

But, also, he has a message for university men. I have two letters before me from undergraduate friends of his from which I want to quote:

"One evening I was asked to the room of ——— (Hopeful). He began telling us stories. I always enjoy stories, but these were of a different kind from any I had ever heard. They were about how interesting sinners can become compelling saints. I listened till after midnight. I had some problems myself, and I wanted to hear still more. We went into his room. He gave me the four absolute principles of Christ: honesty, purity, unselfishness and love, and asked me how my life stacked up beside them. I saw that here was a man who could help me out of my troubles, and I told him all about myself. Next he said:

"'Have you ever surrendered yourself to Christ?' I had not, but I decided that now was the time to do so. The result was such an experience as I had never had before. I lay awake late into the night, thinking of the meaning of what had happened. The new life, with Christ as its centre, is growing all the time. It has taken me out of myself, so that I have gone from a fifth to a third group in my studies. It has cut down my extravagances until with what I am saving I expect to go through a post-graduate course. I have made the most important discovery there is, that Christ was right."

And the other says: " Knowing ———— (Hopeful) has been worth more to me than two and a half years of ————'s professors and books. . . . One morning a little before college opened I met him on the campus, and he asked me to drop down to his house that evening. It was very definitely a turning-point in my life. For the first time here was someone who was willing to sit down and talk with me alone, who somehow knew how to get down to the levels I needed to talk on. I told him many of the things I was ashamed of, which were troubling me, revealing to him my ignorance of the world and of myself. I told him all but one thing. ' Is that all there is to talk about? ' he said. I declared it was. Then in a moment, and in a very friendly way, he said, ' Tom, you lied just now, didn't you? ' How glad I was that he asked, so that I might admit that he was right, and then tell him the whole business. The release and happiness that came to me that night had been unknown before. Later, at a house-party, came another surrender of a boyhood dream of becoming famous: it was not entirely bad, but it was unrelated to my present life, and it was bad *for me*. I shared there also with another fellow in college, and I saw the futility of being educated but with a rotten core inside. ———— (Hopeful) has given of his entire self to me—his house, his food, money, time, thought, care and, best of all, his spiritual vision of what I can become."

It sometimes takes a better thing than a flash of spiritual imagination to see a worker for Christ in a mischievous boy in a juvenile court—it takes everlasting patience, courage, faith to help build that vision into one human character. To this, Hopeful gives his life. Most people would say that a message of conversion, guidance and witnessing for Christ was utterly beyond such lads,—but not Hopeful. With his collegians, it is the same story: neither apathy nor dissipation nor studied scepticism nor fencing about intellectual problems swerves him from an undying faith that the man can and will be delivered from his doubt or need and turned into a force for Christ. There are many to help these boys and men: but not many have I seen who held up to them a living Christ in so winning and yet so exacting a fashion.

I'd rather be behind the times with Hopeful, changing the lives of bad boys and baffled undergraduates, than abreast of them with all the brilliant cynics in the world.

XI

THE SENSITIVE SOUL

PICTURE a small boy awaking to his life in a prosperous middle-class New England town. There are the frame houses, the elm trees, the well-known town-characters, the many churches, the cut-and-dried divisions, the gossip and the tragedies and the excitements. In sight of these, tens of thousands of lives begin and continue and end. Upon the spirit of this boy the more or less isolated life of a small city left its permanent impression.

As a lad, he was almost totally cut off from other boys of his own age. He was an only child, the home was happy and self-sufficient, the mother its sun and spirit. To her he clung always as the one who understood him. There was fear of physical conflict, which made most sports distasteful. There was shyness and desperate reserve, which caused him to walk round the block to avoid having to meet a schoolmate; and which made the school recess a time of inward torment, standing blankly against a wall, suffering as only little boys and girls can suffer, for their suffering is in no wise understood by themselves and most cruelly treated by their fellows.

A boy like this sometimes takes to intellectual or religious things in sheer self-defense. He grows up beyond his equals, and finds his " compensation " in the cultivation of his elders, discussing with them the weighty matters of politics, philosophy and religion, and beginning to use long words which the rest of the boys " would not understand," and would jeer at if they heard them. All this produced a terrific self-centredness—not a deliberate selfishness, but a self-absorption which was unhealthy. Here are the materials for a tragedy of introversion, and but for what later happened this man might have turned into a hopelessly twisted personality.

By the time for high school, this isolation was mitigated by an increasing interest in the social life of those of his own age. The coveted popularity was gained by earning the editorship of the school paper, and was used for the manoeuvering of class elections.

The opening year of the War, he was a Freshman in a university of his own state. He was a green lad, innocent of the knowledge he should have had to go forward in university life with any degree of satisfaction. The year was so full of conflict and incompleteness for him that he decided to change his university, and go to another where the intellectual life was more stimulating, where he might find less need to conform. Still maladjusted as to ordinary social relationships, he plunged more deeply into his books, lectures, music and drama. His innate religious longing was starved in this particular place, where religion was pretty much all rationalized away. So he used to find his way of a Sunday morning to a nearby theological seminary, where the dean was in the habit of preaching fascinating sermons from the chancel steps of his chapel.

Three years later, when the law school was unrewarding, and when his mother's death had made him look life more squarely than ever in the face, he asked himself what it all meant, and as a result of his questioning he entered that seminary as a student. To most outsiders the thought of entering a seminary for theological education is almost as final a step as ordination itself, and pre-supposes some spiritual faith and conviction. But many men come to seminaries as conscious problems, seeking light for themselves as well as for others, and yet uncertain about the future. Oddly enough, sin in an attractive form had never met this young man until now. He got into difficulty. The members of the faculty who were in his confidence dealt with him most kindly and sympathetically, sending him at last to a doctor as the best suggestion they had. "Looking back on it," he says to me, "I can see the pathos of men of God sending me to science for something of which God alone possessed the cure." He assures me that the doctor greatly helped him, but the final power which reached the seat of his motives and transformed his whole outlook was yet to come.

In his Senior year, he had been elected president of the student body. He had wanted to invite Frank Buchman to come and speak to the students, but was advised that this would be unwise. What was his surprise when, one day, the bishop's son, who was also a student at the seminary with him, asked him to come to his room to meet Frank Buchman! "So I went along upstairs," he says, "and laid eyes for the first time upon a countenance which has now become familiar to many in five continents. What I saw was a nose, two eyes and glasses. For the rest, there was the general sense of a shampooed and massaged cleanliness, and a smile of exuberant good nature. He was in process of telling the story of a Chinese lawyer, for the benefit of a friend of mine whose vocation heretofore had been wine, women and song, and who by way of avocation attended the law school."

"As a result of hearing that story," he continues, " the next week-end saw us both at a religious house-party. I was interested and believed in it all. I picked up the language and used the jargon well. I enjoyed myself hugely at the dozen or so other house-parties which I attended during the next two years. But I had not yet gotten consciously sick enough to want the cure. I could and did talk about religion when called upon, but none of it had been allowed to sink down far enough to take root in my life." Then there came ordination and its solemnities, an assistancy in a fine old parish, his marriage, and later on his own church. " Particularly when I got into my own parish," he says, " all that I had gotten at the house-parties slipped away from me entirely. I forsook even the ideal of bringing people to Christ one by one for the mammon of organization and ecclesiastical machinery. I polished my sermons till they shone, but I left individuals without the pale, except as I met them in the course of routine visiting. I shocked some of my conservative parishioners by what were to them novelties, in the way of ritual and doctrine. But I did not shock them by introducing them to the possibility of a vital religious experience in their own lives."

He was invited to attend a meeting of preachers in Washington, who were invited because of unusual possibilities in preaching for a time of intensive training. At one of the services he was chosen to preach, and I never listened to more wordy oratory in my life than that which marked his sermon. He was professional, shy, growingly ecclesiastical, but seemed to me still wistful. We had some long talks together again. Deep down in his life he believed in the things we stood for. When I needed another assistant in the fall, he was called to Calvary.

" It is at Calvary," he says, " that I have had revealed to me the ephemeral nature of my previous religious experience. The major things which have kept me from spiritual release and power have not been gross sins, but insidious sins of jealousy and pride. I have been jealous of the rector, and jealous of the senior assistant. They were both more spiritually effective persons than I, and it hurt my pride to know it and to look for the reason. I would not face it. Finally, in a mood of terrific resentment and rebellion, I resigned, at a most inconvenient time just as the rector was sailing for Europe. I wanted to go at once.

" Now, there is on the staff at Calvary a man of limited education but of amazing perception, the superintendent of our rescue mission. The morning after I had written my resignation he was guided in prayer to come in and see me. He stood in my doorway, and said nothing. In his face was nothing of reproach or judgment, but something unbelievably loving and redemptive: it was a reminder of the face of Christ when He said to Peter, ' Simon, I have prayed for thee that thy faith fail not, and when thou art converted, strengthen thy brethren.' Something inside me melted and broke loose like a dam. I confessed my sins of pride and jealousy and dislike. Then I went and confessed it to the other people with whom I was working. I withdrew my resignation, and willingly continued on the staff. Resentment and hate, in a nature like mine, are not quickly turned into love and fellowship. The crowning of this whole experience came later in a deep spiritual love which God has made it possible for me to feel towards these very people who were once the objects of my jealousy and bitterness. It was given to me in a memorable Communion service as we all knelt together before the altar."

Only those who work with such a sensitive and meteoric personality as this know how deep is its instability, and know also what force lies hidden away beneath its sensitiveness, if only that force can be fully possessed by God. The quality of sensitiveness may be good or bad, according as it means touchy, peevish, personal reactions to situations and life, or on the other hand may mean exquisite understanding of the other lives about it—whether, in brief, it is imprisoned by looking within, or whether by grace it is liberated into looking without. So long as the life is preoccupied with its own problems, antipathies, moods, it will be bumptious, critical, insensitive, defiant—anything to make up for its conscious inferiorities and maladjustments. But when the releasing honesty of facing its failures and faults has been given, and the worst is known and accepted and then surrendered to God, the whole flavour of living is changed. No longer is one himself the emotional centre of all things, taking everything as personal to himself, but he begins to live most fully in the problems and remaking of other personalities. Here is found a reason and a use for all the suffering through which one has passed: it is to be used in understanding and helping others. Here is a spiritual call and commission which is also a perfect psychological sublimation.

Some time after all this had happened, giving a long enough interval to know that it was permanent, a call came from a parish in a small town a hundred miles

away to send a group for several days of personal
witness in the church, and in informal groups outside.
The leading came clearly that the Sensitive Soul should
lead the group, and that he should take with him a
woman parishioner of leisure and means, our parish
secretary, the deaconess of another city parish who
had found new life in her work through the Thursday
evening meetings, the wife of a cost-accountant in Jer-
sey City, and our own sexton whose surrender had
come last fall after " three and a half years of looking
you people over to see if it was real." The local rector
had wanted me to lead the group myself, and at the
station was somewhat shocked at this horde of non-
descripts! He aired his objections in a meeting, and
told some of the group privately at the close of their
stay that he had thought nothing could happen as
things were. This is not just the atmosphere in which
a Sensitive Soul is likely to be successful at leading his
first informal evangelistic campaign! But, nothing
daunted, he quietly set about getting peoples' confidence. Each morning there was a Quiet Time, in
which the whole group, including the rector, the Presbyterian minister and other interested people, came
together to seek " orders " for the day. There were
various groups held, in which stories were told. The
wife of one of the local ministers was touched by one
of the women, and went home to make her surrender
to Christ with her own husband. The wife of one of
the vestrymen made her decision with the woman of
leisure. The Sensitive Soul himself was led in a meeting to tell the story of a remarkable time we had
recently with our choir, where misunderstandings were
so frankly aired and clearly cured, and where such a
spirit of love marked the close of the gathering, that

we felt we had undergone a miniature Pentecost. After this meeting he walked away with a business man who sang in the local choir, and his decision was made. The sexton led a group of boys, told of his own deliverance from drink, explained how God's guidance would make it unnecessary to get into the kind of scrapes which often wrecked young men's lives, had a Quiet Time with them then and there, and then tied up his ends by going to the Presbyterian minister, to whose church most of the boys belonged, and asking him to be sure and have regular Quiet Times with these boys, keep them up to it, and make them forces for Christ! Later on, the rector himself came down to see us, to tell us of how many people had been reached, some of whom he had been after for years, and to thank us for sending such an unlikely set of workers! Back of this effort the Sensitive Soul was the steady, guiding hand, planning the meetings, making the right connections between people, handling the uneasy rector, holding the reins lightly but dexterously in his hands.

Doubtless a great deal was done for the parish and the community and the rest of the workers—but the most obvious benefit, as I saw it, lay in the life of the Sensitive Soul himself. It had been proven to him by what happened, not only that he could win one life to decision for Christ, but that he could handle the much more complex problem of leading a team of workers and helping them to function at maximum. The effect on himself was the establishment of such confidence in God that he forgot his ordinary lack of confidence in himself. Thus it is that men come to spiritual maturity.

While in seminary he had been introduced to the

family of one of our missionary bishops, a family
which numbers seven in all. Six of that family had
entered into a religious experience of such deep and
transforming nature as to completely alter their lives
or immeasurably to enrich them. The head of this
family, as deeply revered and beloved a man as I have
ever known, has found in the religious experience
which has come to his eldest son, a further and fresh
revelation of the power of the Christian Gospel to
make men " to be of one mind in an house." The
youngest son has for several years been groping for
such an experience as came to his brother, disturbed
by a problem for which he could find no solution.
Crippling inhibitions and fears have kept him from
talking frankly with someone who could meet his need.
While this youngster was staying at Calvary House,
the Sensitive Soul met him for the first time, but paid
little attention to him, thinking he was being looked
after by others; besides, he was himself just going off
for a summer vacation and was busy packing. He was
to have left on a Friday, but being needed on Sunday,
decided to stay over. The missionary's son had expected to spend the week-end out of town, but plans
had miscarried. Going out for a quick luncheon alone
on Saturday, the Sensitive Soul had clear guidance to
ask the boy to come along. He disobeyed, got as far
as the street corner, and was arrested by such a compelling conviction to turn back that he could no longer
resist. The result was that within a few moments
they were sitting at lunch together, packing was forgotten, and they were soon in the midst of a real talk.
The boy was ready to make his decision for Christ;
but first there must be gotten into the open what was
involved in that great decision, and for two hours they

talked intimately, after which there was prayer and the decision was made. The first guidance which came to him after his decision was to send two messages, one a cable to his father and mother in a far distant land, and another a radiogram to his brother on the high seas bound on a missionary journey. " I shall never forget the light in his face," says the Sensitive Soul, " and the ring in his voice as we framed these messages together." The reply from his brother was laconic, and told in four words the spiritual history of the whole family: " Now we are seven."

Any Thursday night after the meeting you will see little knots of people talking together in various corners of the hall—some chatting lightly about " what a wonderful meeting it was," but others down at rock-bottom deciding the issues of life. The Sensitive Soul is often the human centre of one of these groups of two or three. Gloriously and at long last, he has gotten out of himself. His life is free and gay for the first time. The old moods, of course, come back momentarily, but he knows what to do with them. Intelligently, sympathetically he is living his life out into other lives. His own problems and their solution form the basis and ground-work of his message. His understanding and sympathy have been distilled out of his old sufferings transfigured by a growing experience of Jesus Christ.

XII

FROM THE FAR COUNTRY

IT is sometimes a tonic thing, in the midst of the soft children of our over-civilized generation, to come upon a born fighter. The story which is to follow concerns a man whose every faculty is nerved for combat. David Harum said that some folks have more human nature than others: some of us, too, inherit more of the instinct of pugnacity from our not very remote ancestors who wandered about in the woods of northern Europe and made their way by their fists. Of course, this tingle in our blood is just raw energy. It can be put anywhere. Whether it is to find its outlet in the stupid waste of war, or in the refined struggle of competitive industry—or whether it can find William James' desideratum, " the moral equivalent for war," depends upon the good sense and the imagination of parents, educators and surrounding society. Formal, inexpensive, listless religion cannot possibly have the slightest attraction for a man like this—he must have a battle, or he will go elsewhere and find one.

He comes of cultivated, well-to-do people. His father was vice-president of one of the great cotton textile plants of the south, and a solid member of the Methodist Church, who brought many ministers and missionaries to his house. His wife entered fully into the church and social life of the city where she lives, centering her effort in her home and her boys, and giving them the best there was. This son went to the conventional preparatory school, and in his graduating year the war broke out: the day President Wilson called for volunteers, he joined the Twenty-ninth Division of Field Artillery, and saw fourteen months of service in France.

He was then but seventeen. He found himself amongst older men, and lost no time catching up to the dissipations which they enjoyed. Completely, prodigally, with abandon, he went the pace. This man does nothing by halves. He came back shot to pieces morally, and entered a university. Besides his studies, he took a job as detective at a race-track, and did a good deal of very good boxing as well: the combination was too much for his academic work, which all seemed appallingly tame in contrast, and at the end of his first year he was dropped. He tried again the following year, but by the middle of that year he had gotten into such a serious scrape that he had to leave home altogether. He went to California and worked for the Standard Oil, and in a few months was in a gasoline plant in Oklahoma. Liquor was the opening wedge for growing dissipation, and he decided that he would quit the country. So he signed up on a steamer bound for the Orient. As she touched at eight seaports en route to Shanghai, he found conveniently accessible to him all the time-worn wares which sin has to offer: he had a fling at the dives in all these port cities. In San Francisco he was promoted to wheelman.

" On this ship was a welterweight prize-fighter," he says, " and we got to be very good friends. At a masked ball in Honolulu a sporting promoter from Manila got drunk and fell on the deck near my post.

Jimmy and I carried him to a stateroom, and the following day he offered us the opportunity to box in Manila. The ship stopped at several Japanese ports, and at Shanghai—and then we jumped the boat at the Philippines. We started training at once and at one of our workouts a prominent manager in the Philippines offered me a contract to fight under his management. I took the name of Teddy Burns of San Francisco. During the fights there I got a very bad eye injury which would not heal in that climate, and I was forced to return to the States. When I reached San Francisco, I was absolutely broke, and went into a regular bum's existence, working in restaurants as a dishwasher and taking anything that would stand between me and starvation. I slept in the park, and later got a cot in the Salvation Army Mission for five cents a night."

During all this time his mother had never wholly lost hope nor ceased to pray that he would give up the life he was living. Now she wrote him to come home. He was given another chance at college, and for three more years continued the same reckless, wild career, constantly exposing his family to worry and anxiety. Leaving the university again, he went into business, where he was successful for a time. But more money meant more dissipation, and he drifted from one position to another. His mother took him on a Mediterranean cruise and through Europe, and he was even blessed by the Pope. Coming home, he tried the hotel business, and his energy soon made him the youngest hotel manager in New York. But he was still the slave of his thirst for liquor and dissipation, and decided to quit work entirely and live by his wits. He carried a gun quite frequently, and narrowly missed paying the extreme penalty of the law on several occasions. He stopped at nothing.

His father had died, but his mother kept on believing he could be changed. Some of us had come to know her about this time, and when she spoke about this wayward son, it made us think of Monica, the mother of St. Augustine, who went to a priest begging him to reclaim her boy: and he said to her, " Go thy ways, and God bless thee, for it is not possible that the son of these tears should perish."

Coming to New York, he was offered a good position with a sales organization if only he could put up a certain amount of capital. Wishing this junior executive position, he turned again to his family for financial help. " The house-party at Minnewaska was then going on," he says, " and with the one intention of getting a loan from mother, I went up for the week-end. I was immediately interested in the type of person and the manner of life which I sensed in this group from every section of society. The ministers did not interest me, because I looked on them as professional good people: but I came in contact with a business man who was a former Broadway star, who told me of his own turn to Christ; and this so convicted me that I longed for the kind of life which I saw about me. I got down on my knees for the first time in many years. I went to the man who was leading the group, and made to him a complete confession of all my past life. In order to leave nothing undone in the attempt to make things right with people I had wronged, I wrote fourteen letters of confession of specific wrong. Without exception, they all forgave me and wished me well in my new life."

Now, every man who breaks with his past, and sets

out to live a new life which is focussed in a totally new
set of values, needs constant help, direction, fellowship
and activity.   The one most important thing in the
world is that he should be grounded solidly in what is
bound to be at the first a more or less emotional aspiration.   We are all aware that this is where much evangelism has failed, where great public efforts which are
not undergirded with personal dealing are always
bound to fail: we are conscious of the need for
" follow-up."   The pity is that it is often those who
care most who yet make follow-up most difficult.   A
family often wants this brand-new boy or girl quickly
delivered at home a completely finished product, un-
mindful that they have failed to produce this change
themselves, and that unless a new spirit is brought in
by steady fellowship to infect these old surroundings,
they have a sullen undertow towards the old life.
Friends often demand that a new-born life should at
once become hard-working, dependable, moodless, settled—which is, of course, to expect a convalescent to
play football.   Even ministers often ask for immediate
conformity, membership, support, forgetful of their
own failure in these lives, and unaware of the many
steps which come first before anything like interest in
the institution of the church should even be mentioned.
This is a good time for interested meddlers to keep
out, unless they will co-operate, and let those who
have, under God, been responsible for the change
sustain it.

The beginning of a daily habit of Quiet Time is perhaps the crucial point in maintaining the new life.   But
the guidance which comes at such times presents its
own problems: and these need to be threshed honestly
with those who are spiritually further along.   Fellow-

ship in a group of believers, each sustaining the other, honest sharing, are needful if the experience is not to die in isolation, or, if it persists, be warped through individualism. But one of the chief needs is that this life should express itself in the lives of others. As Frank Buchman often says, " No man can maintain a growing experience of Jesus Christ whose life does not have an intelligent expressional activity." To take a life lighted at the fire of Christ, and expect to feed that fire by cool, humanitarian efforts is to court failure: to put a man such as we have been describing to teaching boys to play basketball, or raising money for a hospital, or working in a settlement where religion cannot be mentioned, and to think that thereby his spiritual life will be sustained, is to help him back into the abyss. He needs *spiritual* service, he needs to be helped to give to other men what he has been given. Apart from what it will mean to them, let us think now of what it will mean to him. One needs hardly labour the great point contained in the remark of Novalis,* " It is certain my belief gains quite infinitely the moment I can convince another mind thereof."

And so, with the fullest consent and co-operation of his mother, this man was taken into a little group of men and women who were to spend that summer travelling and working for Christ in many different centres, speaking informally to invited people in houses, and working with individuals. All the values of continuance would be thus conserved. In his times of critical temptation, he would be surrounded by those who knew of his struggles and would understand and sustain him. His questions could be answered,

---

* Quoted by Carlyle, *Sartor Resartus.*

his moods of rebellion and slipping, bound to come to
us all, could be dealt with. But chiefly he could begin
an active witness under the direction of those who
knew how to do it.

A very short time after his own conversion, he was
asked to go and see a man in Boston who was suffering
from the after-agonies of drink at the time. This man
came of people of great refinement and wealth, he had
begun to drink during the war, he had married and
lost his wife, and drink was the only way he knew in
which he could drown the sense of futility and emptiness of his life. Medicine and psychiatry had helped,
but they seemed unable to get at the root-motives
which would give the man the desire to change, coupled
with hope about himself. He was in the care of a male
nurse, when " From the Far Country " first saw him.
He talked with him a little at a time, as he was able
and ready to listen to a story, the forepart of which
was so much like his own. He was persuaded to come
to a house-party which was being held at Narragansett
Pier. There he met the Militant Mystic and several
other men who were trying to live the Christian life.
He liked them. One day when almost crying for
another drink, " From the Far Country," who had been
the custodian of his bottle and given him a drink when
it was medically necessary (think of this man, himself
a drunkard less than a month before!) said to him
lovingly and firmly, " No, old man. We are through
with that now. We are going to get down on our knees
and ask God to take away the craving." Three of
them knelt down. The third man prayed aloud, very
simply, very sincerely. It shook the man they wanted
to reach, to the bottom of his soul. He made his
decision for Christ. Today he is a victorious spirit,

giving his life to winning men, and is on a mission to university students in South Africa as this book goes to the publisher.

As the summer went on, " From the Far Country " realized that at last he was at home, that he had found the career God had dreamed for him when he was created. Life after life that summer he saw changed, —deep, inward, unsensational changes which made for them a new heaven and a new earth. His own spirit, spite of fightings and occasional fears, grew stronger. The thing was not a chimera, or some other man's hope, but God's sure way to life. He was still young, he had seen " the other side," he had tried both ways and there was no comparison. Why not give his life to it full-time? No one urged it on him; in his soul, fertilized with fresh experiences, it grew. And so this man who three months before had despised ministers, was confirmed and sought entrance into the ministry. He went to a seminary for his training, and kept in touch with the group that had won him.

Towards the middle of the year I had a letter from him which ran thus: " Last Thursday I had my first experience of compelling guidance. God plainly said to me, ' Go down on the green and preach.' It kept coming, so I started down, but lost my nerve and turned back. On thinking it over, I saw it was deep ingratitude, so I went down, stood at the fountain and began to talk about Jesus. About twenty people stopped. One man came afterwards to talk about his problem and has been to our chapel twice since. Every day interviews come. Yesterday an old lady handed up a note which asked me to come and see her son. I found him a nervous case, in bed and irritable. She told me she didn't go to her rector because she did not

think he cared much about visiting the sick. Maybe
this is unfair: but then again, something is wrong when
the relation of a minister to his people is so formal
that one of them hesitates to ask him to go and see a
sick boy."

This kind of work is too unconventional to draw
no fire, and one day came an appeal: " Please pray
hard for me. I am running the gamut of criticism
from those about me, and know what it is to feel a
knife in the back. I must love everyone, and know
how you and Frank must have suffered. It's all for
the cause, though, so why should I worry? I would
like to clean up a couple of these underhanded birds,
but the days of hit-and-run are gone." One wishes
that it were possible to say something to the conventional Christians about the way they do not hesitate
to quench smoking flax like this. Maybe he is young,
maybe he is green and inexperienced and a bit crude
in some of the things he says. Have you got his
Gospel? Have you got his nerve? Have you anything that would have saved him in the first place?
Do you know that Jesus was talking about such as he
when He said that you had better have a millstone
about your neck and be cast into the sea than that
you should be an offense to one of these little ones,
these babes in the new life, who are such a shocking
challenge to the moss-grown conventionals who are
sometimes their wise superiors?

All this past summer he has been talking over a
loud-speaker outside our church, at noon and at five
o'clock, using other men and women to give their own
witness of Christ, and speaking himself. When he is
through, he goes out on the street, and talks to individuals. Many of them tell him their troubles.

"One factory hand came and said he was in deep trouble: a few days later he made a full confession and decision for Christ. He went to his own minister and volunteered for any kind of activity where he could be useful. He told me a few weeks later that he had never known such happiness, and that God had taken out of his life the main besetting sin which had defeated him for years." He has spoken in jails, penitentiaries, missions and various clubs, always giving to men his own powerful story of what Christ has done for him. Sometimes as he speaks, I am reminded of Richter's saying about Martin Luther, "His words are half-battles."

As I think about him, the thing which impresses me most is the way in which Christ has taken hold of his obvious instinct for the fight, redeemed it and redirected it, trained it upon real and not upon imaginary or deliberately provoked enemies, and through this very warfare given to him a service in which is his own surest peace. You feel every talent, every energy, every nerve, bend in this supreme and superb conflict to rescue the lives of men from sin, degradation and futility. He would never have given a moment's attention to tame and timid religion; but he is giving his life to strenuous and demanding and romantic religion. I wish that some of the bored and jaded members of our modern society, so wasting for a new thrill, might keep company with this man long enough to see the obvious joy which he finds in his high conflict, and throw themselves into it with him. No wonder men like this have dodged religion and the ministry, when it has been put before them in terms of timidity, and conformity, "haziness and happy thoughts." This kind of man has to have something to dig his teeth into, something to capture every waking thought and stretch every nerve. Thank God, in *this* kind of ministry he has it.

But there is something deeper than just the glory of a fight. This would soon wear itself out in hard contention and drive people away. " I am sure," he wrote me months ago, " that we can win over our opponents by more love and less pounding dogmatism. I feel convicted about my own bulldog tactics, and am going to start on loving lines." He has started " on loving lines." You feel it in his spiritual victories where men are won, you feel it still more in his spiritual failures where they are not won—a tender love for human lives, a compassion for the unshepherded multitude like unto One who loved them long ago and loves them still. This man might have written the words of John Bunyan: " In my preaching I have really been in pain, and have, as it were, travailed to bring forth children to God; neither could I be satisfied unless some fruits did appear in my work. If I were fruitless, it mattered not who commended me; but if I were fruitful, I care not who did condemn."

XIII

TRIPLE FIRST

IT is a common opinion that an evangelical movement, which wears an emotional aspect to the
average man, may succeed in picking up the lame
ducks, the maladjusted, the emotionally suggestible,
the gullibles generally, but that it cannot command the
attention of the competent, the thoughtful, the sufficient, especially of the intellectually brilliant. If these
are ever drawn into the service of religion, it is thought
that this must be in the period when a movement has
cooled down, grown respectable, and can offer a field
of service to a moderate and intelligent person. How
unfair and ungrounded is this notion will be suggested
by the inclusion within this book of a man who graduated with exceptional honours from one of the admit-
tedly most intellectual colleges of Oxford University.

In Oxford those who take the final examinations are
graded in classes. To be a " first " is to be in the best
possible grade. During one's whole career in Oxford
one only takes two examinations ordinarily, a preliminary and a final. The preliminary usually comes
at the end of the first year, and only qualifies one to
go on to an " honour's school." But for those taking
" greats," a school of classical philosophy, history and
languages, the preliminary examination may be a
rather bigger thing, and is called " honour moder-
ations," or in slang, " honour mods." It consists

mostly in pure classical scholarship, and for it a
" class " is awarded. The subject of this story took
these two " schools," honour mods and greats, and
achieved a first in each—which makes a Double First.
He was then a B.A., but was entitled to read a further
" school." He took theology, and in it gained another
First, which made him a Triple First, " as you may
imagine," declares my Oxford informant in these
technical matters, " a rare specimen."

His father was a clergyman, a leading member of
the Evangelical party of the Church of England, and
later a bishop. He met his wife when they were workers in a mission in one of the industrial cities, and
their united consecration to the work of the Church
gave the flavour of their home and the atmosphere in
which their children were reared—" a truly Christian
atmosphere," declares Triple First, " which always
held us, though we did not always realize all that
it meant."

At school he was a great intellectual success, and
enjoyed the friendship of a real Christian who was his
housemaster, and an old friend of his family's. Confirmation came at fifteen, and he identifies with it his
" moral conversion "—his " spiritual conversion " did
not come until later—though he had not gone very far
wrong, he was, he says, " just beginning to gather
impetus on the downward slope." There was also, as
an anchor, the quiet influence of a Senior with whom
he shared a study. During his last year, he was head
of the school and of his house, and thus had a good
deal of responsibility, and realized it with that solemn
sincerity of schoolboys. " My values," he says, " were
definitely Christian, but I was not wholly converted.
I had my doubts and questioned much, but would gen-

erally defend the Christian position. I do not feel
that I ever let my scepticism get to the very bottom
of me: but I had periods of intense depression, and
once was half-tempted to end it all."

In 1921 he went up to Oxford, where he declares
that he " was rather agreeably surprised to find that
quite prominent athletes took religion as a reality.
Many of the ex-war men were still up. I gladly entered the Student Christian Movement, and though the
evangelical society of the time did not particularly
attract me, I readily accepted an invitation to go to
the Keswick Convention of 1922, for ' Keswick ' was
a word of happy associations in my home."

" In the company which attended the Convention
from Oxford, composed of seventeen undergraduates
and young graduates, I found something that I had
never found before. I there made friends with ' The
College Chaplain,' and ' Joculator Domini,' and another
man, none of whom I had ever seen before, but who
have become three of the greatest friends of my life.
Frank Buchman came to the house-party one night.
His visit meant new birth to at least two of the men.
But personally I was prejudiced against him by what
I had heard. My source of information was not an
impartial one, I am afraid. To me the challenge came
the following night when the Chaplain General, who
was there also, took prayers after supper. I realized
then that the price of peace and power was summed
up in surrender on the question of purity, and I made
the surrender vocally and definitely in the concluding
time of extempore prayer. That was the decisive
moment in the long process of my conversion.

" My first real contact with Frank Buchman was at
Keswick a year later. My life had not been consis-

tently on the highest level during the intervening year. It seemed right to share that with him, and also to tell him of my original prejudices against him—this came in the course of a long Quiet Time in St. John's Church, after one of the morning Bible readings. When I went to him, Frank Buchman was his usual cheerful, helpful, prayerful self, and I don't think that more need be said."

Now the problem with a man like this is not only "moral," in the broad sense; it is also dispositional. He faces not only the common problems of inner conflict which disturb us all, but his very intellectuality may be a wall between him and common men, and it may be also a refuge into which he retreats away from human reality. There is an undertow towards books, in a life like this, which *may* be as destructive of the highest usefulness as a taste for gin, or a temper of laziness. Here is a scholar, a brilliant and gifted man, headed for the ministry of the Church. Whether he is to be expert in ancient facts, but incapable of ferreting out present facts about human lives, depends upon whether or not he meets a man who knows human beings, as well as Christ, and who will keep hammering it into him that scholarship divorced from life is only a partial blessing. While there is so much talk about scholarship, might there not be more talk about scholarship in human lives, so that a parson may know something beside the ingredients of his Gospel, and be familiar with the reactions of ordinary men? One wants to save ministers from this deadly, insulating detachment as much as he wants to save them from their sins! For if we truly define sin as " anything that walls us off from God, or from other people," then self-consciousness and discomfort in the presence of sinners and pagans and unbelievers is a real sin, and has got to go as any other sin.

For some time he was more or less out of touch with the Movement. He was quietly pursuing his studies, and was ordained in 1926, and remained on as chaplain of one of the theological colleges at Oxford. This latter had been a hard decision for him: because his old school had invited him to come back and teach classics, and he very much wanted to go. He realized that to do so would be selfish, and would cut him off from the largest possible service to the Kingdom of God. He was also made chaplain of one of the colleges. But between official appointment to these offices, and a genuine message for the men whose lives one brushes day by day, there may be a great gulf fixed.

" Fellowship with the Group," he says, " has kept the highest steadily before my eyes, and when I have failed, I have been enabled to realize it pretty quickly. I am coming more and more to realize the worth of fellowship, and the price of having it,—also to realize that ' two are better than one,' that it is the team and not the individual which has the better chance of success; and that is a good thing for a sceptical individualist like me to learn." There are plenty of scholars of Church history who know all that in the abstract, yet who concretely never get away from their own inveterate individualism or learn to merge their own experience and activity with others whose knowledge and experience will challenge and perhaps modify their own. It is much easier to study St. Francis' movement, or John Tauler's, or George Fox's, than it is to throw oneself into a contemporary movement which is in its initial stages, whose final outcome is not certain, and which tests the faith of its participants all the time. One needs hardly to say that self-identification with a modern movement, which raises real issues and challenges so much in contemporary religious activity, is harder for such a man as we are describing than for almost any other type. The intellectual, of all men, finds it most distasteful to lose himself in a movement where the intuitional emphasis is deep, and to become one of a functioning group bent on definite evangelism.

" Further," he adds, " my university work, on its intellectual side (though I loathe such distinctions—all work is spiritual), is theological; and the Fellowship has kept my theology in touch with life. The real fruits of that will probably be reaped twenty years from now, if the books I feel that I must one day write are ever written. In one sense, a ' Don ' is not an ordinary minister, and a College Chaplain who is also a teacher must needs live a kind of ' double life.' At the same time, he has got to unify these two lines of effort. I do not claim to have succeeded, but I do believe that I am on the right lines. Theology, instead of being the dead thing some people suppose it to be, is charged with life; without it the Church would be dead in a generation, or lost in a maze of speculation. But, equally, theology depends on experience, first of God; and then of, with and through other men and women."

A man with such a wide knowledge of the Church's past with a keen eye for unrealities and blind alleys, with such profound knowledge of what men have thought and said and decided in the past, on theological and ecclesiastical matters, is bound to be of immense usefulness to a movement in its early stages. Again and again, in small or large groups, or individually, he is asked for light upon doctrinal or philo‹

sophical points, and he is invariably prepared to give the results of his thought and study in simple, direct, helpful ways. He has done and is doing a great service for the movement by his penetrating intellectual powers. Says a man just out of Oxford University, " He has helped as a steadying influence on the Oxford work. His loyalty has been constant, and his identification with the work has helped in many quarters. Also his knowledge of past history and controversies has been a great help."

In writing to an American bishop concerning the larger aspects of the movement as it has affected the undergraduates at Oxford, he has this to say: " I feel that this work is making a real contribution to the Christian life of this generation, and that it challenges us all to a more vital witness for our Lord. The ' Groups,' as we call them in Oxford, are touching men whom ordinary pastoral methods do not reach, in particular the athletic ' tough.' The free and unconventional, and at the same time intensely sincere atmosphere of the ' Groups,' and still more of a house-party, is acceptable to the modern mind, and so is the frank facing of sexual difficulties, as opposed to the ' hush, hush ' methods of the past. In the challenge to a full surrender of the whole personality to Jesus Christ, and in the insistence upon discipline, especially the ' Morning Watch ' or ' Quiet Time,' there is nothing which is not in accord with all that is best in our ecclesiastical history and heritage. I believe that men and women of today are really (if often unconsciously) hungry for the unification of life which acceptance of these standards always brings."

XIV

CONCLUSION—HOW SHALL I BEGIN?

IT may be that some who will read the stories in this book would like to know how this whole message might be made effective in their own lives and churches. We are not talking about an ecclesiastical method, but about a life: and while life is dynamic and definite enough, nobody has ever defined it. I do not propose now to write an exhaustive treatise even on my own conception of practical religious work, but merely to say something of how you might begin.

At the outset I ask you to put as far as possible from your mind that you want to " get the knack." There is no trick about this message, no knowledge of psychology or human nature, which alone can enable you to grasp the meaning and force of it. I used to think that if only I could hide behind a curtain while some master of the art of working with individuals was " operating," I could catch the hang of it and begin to do it myself. But the spirit and power of this message is essentially a thing to be caught by spiritual fellowship, and by the guidance of the Holy Spirit, and not by imitation or study. I feel a real danger that people will think they understand the movement because they have read about it: nobody understands it until he experiences something of what lies behind the verse in the First Epistle of St. John: " That which we have seen and heard declare we unto you, that ye also may have fellowship with us: and truly our fellowship is with the Father, and with His Son Jesus Christ." The true exegesis of that verse is not found in Bible commentaries, but in a working fellowship of witnessing Christians.

I have long since ceased to believe that " influence " was sufficient by itself to win other people for Christ; but there is this much force in it, that no man can win others to a life he is not living himself. I know a good many parsons who wonder why their people do not live robust spiritual lives, when they are themselves rather tame specimens of apostles. We need first of all to ask whether we are in any position to attempt to transmit a living experience of Christ to others.

I never learned more about religious work than I learned from Frank Buchman when he said, " The first and fundamental need is ourselves." It is so much easier to skip this first requirement, and go on to ask what comes next. The whole process has got to begin with us. For a good many it must begin with a fresh sense of sin, and we might safely question ourselves about professional ambition, discouragement and self-pity, grudges against authorities or members of our congregation, our dispositions at home, physical and intellectual laziness, intemperance, sins of the flesh and of the mind, compromise in preaching, want of private prayer and Bible study, favouritism, and a spirit of harsh judgment. We shall never do effectual work with other people except as it begins in an experience of our own: and we may need to seek out that honest soul whom we trust more than any one else to say the truth to us, and in the way appropriate to us, make a clean breast of the facts about ourselves, a " confes-

sion," if you call it that, but let there be no spirit of
" Haven't I confessed enough? " for that will defeat
the whole purpose: let it come out, all of it, without
justification or excuse—begin with yourself at rock
bottom, and no pride left.

Then we shall need to make a new surrender which
involves the break with our particular sins, and includes restoration and restitution, confession and forgiveness, where they are necessary. Those times of
self-humiliation are the most unlovely and unwelcome
hours of the Christian life: but they grow power and
joy and peace, as rotten earth grows roses. For some
of us the Christian life has been a long aspiration: now
let it *begin* somewhere in an act of complete, irrevocable self-surrender, with some human witness if that
will give it force. " But I have done that in the past."
Yes, many men have thought they had: but either it
was not comprehensive enough in the beginning or they
revoked the decision, or let it slide through failure to
grow. Let it be thorough this time, and final.

Now the core and centre of the New Life must be
the Holy Spirit. Please do not take this in the merely
theological sense, but simply remember the difference
which He made in the early Church, and study the
Acts to see what He empowered those men and women
to do. G. K. Chesterton says that Christianity con-
centrates on the man at the cross-roads, and the all-
important question is what he is to do next. Most
people " make up their own minds," or fly nervously
to a friend to get advice: how much better to quiet
one's spirit in the presence of God, and wait for the
fulfilment of the promise, " *Unto the godly* there
ariseth up light in the darkness." A good many people have stopped praying, not for any intellectual rea-

sons, but simply because for them nothing happened in prayer: they felt the inappropriateness of merely making suggestions to Almighty God, and they stopped. They might have gone on if we had told them that the most important part of prayer is not what we say, but what we hear—not what we do, but what God does. I am as certain of the reality of God's guidance through the Holy Spirit as I am of my own life: and its validity is ultimately to be tested by its correspondence with the known realities of other experience, and by its growing workability over a long period of time. Now, guidance has got to become concrete and, in the best sense, habitual for ministers. This cannot come true without the setting apart of a definite time in the morning, the very first part of it, for sufficient prayer, Bible study, and listening for the Holy Spirit's directions. Most of us have " drawn a blank " at first, and gone through some awkward spiritual antics: yet that time with God has come to be the heart of our lives, and we have learned to depend upon God's guidance, when we are freed from " wishful thinking " in the matter, as the surest avenue to reality which we possess. Let it be said often, this is no short-cut to truth which we are supposed to dig out with our minds: it is God's crystallization of truth from the facts we have and also from some facts which we cannot possibly *know*, but can only guess by what humanly we call a " flash of intuition." The " guidance " of religion is " intuition " plus. It is not a substitute for, but a tremendous supplement to, the common processes of thought. The sustenance of the new spiritual life lies in the material in the Bible, which is everlasting and universal; and then in God's direct messages to us, which are temporal and personal, but have sometimes widespread effects. Let a man cultivate that time alone with the living God day by day, refusing his newspaper before he has had his Quiet Time, and his conversion has at least one good leg to stand on.

Then we need to win one person. The name may come in guidance, in a persistent " concern "—it may be a parishioner, or an outsider, or a member of the family. What we seek is an appropriate time to tell that person what Christ has done for us, not a long wordy diatribe, but a concrete incident, perhaps the incident of our surrender. The occasion may not come for months, it may come that day. It can never be done until confidence is won, until they and we feel " easy " together. With an outsider, it may involve learning what his interests are, and sharing in them with him until he likes us. He needs to find in us something real, something attractive, very often something *new* which he never saw before, that makes him say to himself, if not aloud, " That man has got something." Now, somewhere the conversation must slip guidedly and naturally round to asking him whether he does not want a richer life, the joy that comes from God. And we must avoid argument like the plague: Joubert says, " We can convince others by our own reasons, but we can persuade them only by theirs." What we want to do first is not to secure agreement with a position, but to whet an appetite. Henry Drummond said that the faculty of the new evangelism was not the reason but the imagination. If fish are not hungry they will not bite: and it is no use to try another bait, or to thrash the water because you want them to bite—the thing is to slip good-naturedly away, and bide your time till a better occasion, and mind the Old Adversary does not tell you that you failed, or

ought to have won him, when possibly under God you
have gone as far as you could at that time. It will be
fatal to go too fast, as fatal as it is in many ministers
to go too slow. Keep sensitive to his appetite, and feed
him no faster than he takes it, always managing not to
" over-sell," and to leave him wanting more.

Some day such a person will open up, or else give
indirect sign that he wants the thing you have. People
express that in curious ways: sometimes by violent
arguments against everything you say, yet they can't
quite let you alone and stay away. When he wants
it, begin to talk about what stands between him and
Christ, as our Lord did with the woman at the well.
Most people are in some kind of moral need, and the
cheerful sentimentality which makes ministers think
themselves helpful when they pat these people on the
back, and compliment them on being so kind and good
and doing so well with their difficulties, is often a sick-
ening betrayal of Christ. Hear this true word from
Karl Barth: " They expect us to understand them better than they understand themselves, and to take them
more seriously than they take themselves. We are
unfeeling, not when we probe deeply into the wound
which they carry when they come to us for healing,
but rather when we pass over it as if we did not know
why they had come." Blind parsons who do not see
what goes on in the community, optimistic parsons who
always think things are better than they are, incompetent parsons who cover up their inability to meet people's deepest needs by pretending they are not there,
have done more than any one else to keep so many
religious people upon a life-long level of mediocrity.
One does not want a heavy, censorious atmosphere,
charged with solemnity: one wants simply a candid

atmosphere, in which together men can face the truth, and find Christ's way out. We have spoken already * of the cleansing, liberating effect of talking with a trusted friend, and opening our whole hearts. This binds into deep fellowship, and establishes the kind of relationship which ideally ought to exist between a pastor and his people. I have seen a good many young ministers establish this kind of real spiritual relationship with someone in their congregation for the first time: and it was as though they felt that *now,* at least, their work had begun. And most often it had been achieved by the willingness of the minister to share his own real self, struggles, sins and all, and to begin, not as a superior or " director," but as an equal,—two honest people in need searching for more of God.

The object of that talk is ultimately to persuade the person to give his life to Christ, as the worker must have done first. It is a wicked thing to bring people so far as honest confession, and not carry them the next step into conversion. Yet many a spiritual talk which has had some costly honesty in it has gone off into vagueness and been sidetracked, because we either did not know how, or did not dare, to ask them to make a real decision. The most helpful thing we can do to make surrender a reality to ordinary people is to help them to itemize surrender: as you have faced the problems together, remember them, and let them head up into one great inclusive decision. It means, of course, giving all their sins and problems to God, taking a different " way " the rest of their lives, and trusting God for all that they cannot see at the time.

* Pages 60–61.

Our own faith that such an act may mean a turning-point for this life will be contagious: one sign of misgiving, or too much preoccupation on our part with the next stages of the struggle, will be enough to prevent a great decision from being made. The average church-member has never been asked to surrender all to Christ, or has never been shown how to do it: that their lives are dead-level and uninspiring is not their fault, but ours. There is not a dull, lack-lustre one of them that cannot shine with joy and be used of God to win other lives, if we will but learn how to help them and give them the requisite time. I have seen too many types find the fullness of this joy to put it outside the reach or capacities of anybody. And it will not always be the " likely " person that will do the best work.

" Yes, that is all very well," you say, " but what comes next? There are plenty of good beginners. But they fall down on perseverance." Precisely. Now, the first reason why they give up is that they never got decisively started. Your confirmation candidates grew cold because they never got thoroughly warm: they meant it, yes, but they were not converted to Christ, because you did not show them what was involved in their surrender to Him, and help them one by one to make that surrender. Nobody can effectually continue what he never decisively began. The fault was a poor start nine times in ten. Just here lies the worst failure of ministers after there has been a preaching-mission in their churches: they have no idea what to do with an enthusiastic new-born Christian. I had a mission some time ago in a man's church, and afterwards he told somebody " the meetings didn't last." Bless his heart, no wonder they didn't last—he hadn't the ghost of a notion how to keep the people going who were touched! The average man of this kind wants to break spiritual colts to the harness of the established church machinery, and they either succumb and yield too readily for their own soul's good, or else they balk and the parson is through with them. There is not much spiritual " continuance " in the ordinary altar-guild, or church society, or even the average service. *Something has happened to these people, and they think it ought to happen to other people, and they miss something in most church-members, and they are stirred, and they need the companionship of other souls on fire.* Sometimes I see a vital, high-stepping sinner converted who all his life has done things in the grand manner, sinned with abandon, lived expansively and without restraint—do I want him to look like a church-member twelve months from now? No, I don't. I don't want to tame him for a single minute: I want all that dare and swing and freedom to be used for God. He may not make a very good vestryman, or delegate to diocesan convention just yet, but he can get hold of that drunk down in the village, and he can catch the attention of people the vestrymen don't touch, and he can make religion a live issue with the very people who say it's as dead as a door-nail. A lot of our church fare is not gauged to athletes, but to invalids—it's all so desperately mild. People that have been converted need study, but it must be *live* study, that feeds their imaginations and helps them in working for others. They need prayer, but it must be living prayer in which things take place: guidance is adventurous, even when it refers to home-drudgery or church responsibilities, and it feeds the fires of faith. They need worship, but they will find that out down the trail a bit much better than they will at the beginning. Don't smother a new convert with all the safeguards the church has found valuable as an offset to enthusiasm, or you'll probably put out the fire altogether!

Now, the greatest help in continuance, next to vital Quiet Times, is a sharing fellowship. It must be made up of like-minded people. It may begin with you and one other person. I made a fatal mistake in forming our first group at Calvary, by throwing the invitation open to everybody: about thirty came, and I did all the talking because none of them had had a vital experience, and after three months, I knocked the thing in the head and began over again. The group must begin with converted people. You want time for united Quiet. You want time for sharing up-to-date. And you will talk about working with other people. As others are won, they will be brought into the group, and occasionally some may be brought in before they are won, provided you are sure they won't run away with the meeting, and that there are enough people there who are really won to set and maintain the level of reality. Gradually enough people are won to ensure real testimonies and to follow any unreal talk from a newcomer by a strong, guided witness. These meetings, held perhaps weekly, are kept fresh and vital by the testimonies of new people, and by new experiences of those who have been won. There is no place here for the dreary repetition of stale spiritual history, and while you may occasionally draw a shouter, or a quoter of texts and " lovely thoughts," they will usually find the pace a little rapid for them and not come back. If they persist in spoiling your meetings, you may have to tell them to stay away: but we have only had occasion to do that once in three and a half years of our Thursday evening meetings, and once I had to haul a man down for silliness while he was speaking. In such a group the masks are off. People are themselves, and if they pretend to be anything else, they do not fool you for long. Here all the difficulties of the further stages of the journey can be faced frankly together, the dry times, the times of returning temptation, of discouragement, of bafflement over how to win somebody. But the genius of maintaining such a group lies in keeping people moving forward all the time, sharing honestly with somebody right along, and trying to win others: and the genius of conducting such a group lies in ease, naturalness, laughter, freedom from strain, and above all running openness to God's Holy Spirit to tell you what to do next. In course of time it may be inevitable that the meeting should be open to all. Through honest testimony which often touches the concrete details of life, others see their own difficulties mirrored, and find not only that they are not alone in their struggle, but also that there is a solution in a real experience of Jesus Christ. A group like this should raise up leadership from within itself. One man I know, when he accepted another call, left behind him in his parish a group of lay-people which has continued unabated in his absence: lives continue to be changed as a result of the work of that group.

This ought to be the central *activity* of your parish. Worship is, of course, the heart and nerve-centre of it: but in a group like this you will have contact with those not far enough along as yet to know the meaning of worship or Holy Communion. Where there is *life,* there is drawing-power. Such a group might well be held in someone's home, rather than in your own or in the parish house, so as to free it entirely from the prejudice which attaches in the minds of so many to the avowedly ecclesiastical. Here many a tongue-tied church-member learns how to open up for Christ, and many a life that thought the Church was dead and sticky and self-satisfied sees an experience of Christ in understandable terms. Every age, every live movement, every vital church, has made some provision for free spiritual fellowship and exchange: and these have gone dry and dead only when those who attended them began to live in their own spiritual past.

This kind of an activity, if it is put first, frankly commits your church to primarily spiritual service. The monetary, institutional, organizational aspects fall into secondary place, where I believe they belong. Three questions arise in this connection with which I should like to deal separately.

The first is the whole matter of church societies and organizations. No fair-minded judge will deny that a good many of them have outlived their usefulness, and are being continued for the sake of some old people's feelings who have been connected with them for a long time. One man I know went to take a small church and found thirty organizations in full swing! No parish needs so many as that: it means statistics for the year-book, and activity for a few volunteers, but it means duplication and it does not put the Kingdom of God much further ahead. A few ought to be kept on which have a real function, and which mean that certain organizational details of the parish can be committed to responsible and faithful lay-people: but these must fulfil their function as part of a completely spiritualized parish, and if any of them insist upon going their old way, refusing to be transformed into more

usefulness, scrap them. Says H. R. L. Sheppard,*
" It is better, I think, to close down and start something fresh than to go on attempting to lash moribund
guilds, which no one needs, into a mild activity."
These parish organizations would be harmless enough
if they did not each demand something of the minister
which drains him of energy he ought to put somewhere
else: they mean he almost never sees his people except
as chairman of this, or secretary of that; these things
which began as helps have lived on to be hindrances,
and many a clergyman's life is bedevilled by them till
he has no fresh strength to do creative work in his
parish. Organizations which grow out of needs, and
fulfil real functions, are useful: but we would do well
to test them all afresh, and see whether they are mere
appendages which have lost their usefulness. Otherwise, we shall be the slaves of back-breaking ecclesiastical drudgery.

The second question is that of money. It frames
itself something like this: " If I did nothing but evangelistic work, in my own parish and out of it, where
would the support come from? " The answer lies in
a further question, whether God led you where you
are, or whether you went there through ambition, a
larger salary, a more agreeable social life, and without
His guidance. You may need to reinvestigate your
situation, and ask Him whether you are in the right
place. If you are, not only may you safely put spiritual work first, but it may prove to be disastrous, eter-
nally and perhaps temporally considered, if you do not.
There is no more humiliating, unchristian picture in
this world than a minister creeping about amongst his

* *The Human Parson*, p. 89.

people with money everlastingly in his mind. I know the vestry can be taskmasters, and sometimes show little faith: but have you stepped out enough on God's promises to show them spiritual fruits, and *then* asked them to match your works by their faith? I don't always blame vestries for holding a close rein upon a man who is not changing lives: but a man who is helping people to find the Gospel of Jesus Christ will never lack for materials. If people are being deeply helped, money will come from unsuspected quarters. If I may speak from experience, we went into an old parish with a fearfully run-down plant four years ago: and today we have a splendid parish house, the entire church interior has been done over, we have paid our apportionment every year, and while there are some debts outstanding, they were not so large but what a financially wise vestry thought it right we should assume them. We secured our new equipment by appeal from the chancel and a letter to each parishioner which I signed. There was no financial organization. The cost of postage and paper may have been twenty-five dollars. I gave about two solid days of work in all: my secretary gave probably two weeks. No one was dunned. In every pew leaflets were placed, requesting prayer that God's will for our parish be fulfilled. So that now I simply decline to worry about money, though I have a far deeper sense of *my* responsibility about it, together with the vestry, than I had when I went to Calvary. Give people the Gospel, get them converted, and you need not fear but God will provide the means for your work.

A third question concerns adequate leadership. Dealing with people one by one takes enormous time and energy. A minister must study, he must visit, he must give time to sermons and to the parish, and he must exercise and rest. How can he give the required time to individuals? The secret lies in the raising up of a staff of assistants out of those who are being won for Christ. In a certain proportion of the people who are won, leadership will emerge. Of these, a few may have money enough of their own to work as full-time volunteers, as, for instance, seven men and women are doing with us in New York at the present time, without a cent of salary. I have been amazed at the number of people whose attention could not be gotten for little jobs about the church which seemed to accomplish little, but who were open and ready for the investment of their lives. Many a parish, like my own, cannot increase its budget for salaries: but there will often be those who, if fully won for Christ, will give part or full time for service in working with individuals. I believe that the best training for people like this does not lie in courses in social work, or religious education—these may be helpful supplements at some time, but they do not teach workers how to meet people's deepest needs and win them for Christ: the best training will be to let them learn by doing, sending them after someone, and then talking through with them afterwards their approach, etc., until they learn through experience what Drummond called the " rationale " of conversion. One thinks of small parishes, and of the need for a strong women's worker, who can take interviews with women and girls which it is better a woman should take. Now, the temptation on the part of some men who read this will be to speak to some likely lady before she is soundly enough changed to be effective, or can be relied upon intelligently to work with people. It takes time to season people, and premature thrusting of them into leadership will harm them more than help. But we need imagination about such people. This may be a much better way, for instance, to get that promising lad into the ministry than by directly suggesting it: draw him in, teach him how to win people now, and there will come a time when everything else is dull by comparison, and of course he will go into the ministry!

This brings up a further question about the training and work of a staff. Whether the staff be two or twenty, its deepest problem as a staff lies in the relations between its members. I am convinced that most church staffs need pretty thorough house-cleaning: there are often jealousies, misunderstandings, sentimental relationships, and disguised dishonesties between them, and sometimes a complete divorce between the life they live about the church, and that which they live outside. People like this can do the routine work of the church, but they can never draw lives to Christ by their own radiant spiritual joy, because they haven't got any to spare. A church is a failure which is not drawing all its working force, from the janitor to the rector, into a working spiritual unity. Sometimes we inherit workers from a former régime; we need to do all we can to win them for a vital spiritual service, where they are actually winning lives and not only doing routine work, and if they will not come in with us fully, there is no use trying to carry them longer—they will only form a point of disaffection and division. How would your church stand up under the test: are all the employees with you to the hilt in your spiritual programme? I recommend to churches that they find out pretty specifically what impression their employees make upon people—the sexton, the secretary, the parish worker, the clergy. The worst sore-headed bear I have met in the last twelve months was a church-sexton who gave to people who came in anything but a Christian reception. Men like that can be, and need to be converted,—far more than those who have no official attachment to the church. The staff ought to meet often, surely once or twice a week, for unhurried Quiet Time and sharing till the air is clear, before practical work comes up at all. I remember last fall just as we came back from vacation to move into a new parish house, and " things " fairly cried out to be settled, we took the whole first staff meeting of three hours to clear up the relations between ourselves and God, and never touched those other questions till next meeting. In the long run, that sort of thing saves hours of time. It puts first things first, and you get off on the right foot. You need to know these people through and through, and it never does to send them on about their work and only meet them to talk about that: *they* are the problem in their work, as we are in ours. Unity cannot be had by the dominance of the rector: it can only be had by knowing each other all round, and giving each other time enough to develop and maintain a true spiritual fellowship.

*   *   *   *   *   *

One never comes to the end of a book without feeling that he has left unsaid the things which most needed to be said. I believe so profoundly that the Church needs redemption and reawakening, and that this cannot possibly come from any secondary suggestions or remedies, but must begin in the souls of the ministers and leap like fire to the people. Through others, providentially and not of myself, I have discovered something which for me has increased the personal reality of the Lord Jesus Christ, and given me a ministry of joy and adventure. I want other men to have that, especially men who are beaten and discouraged over the wide discrepancy between the Ideal Gospel and the Actual World, and baffled about bringing the two together. We might win back by spiritual power the sons and daughters of our jaded and machine-ridden age whom we have certainly not won by our numerous substitutes for it. It is a serious time. The only thing that can prevent our world from going pagan is a fresh accession of power into the Christian Church. If I have said anything in this book about the Church or my brother-ministers which has seemed harsh or critical to some, I have said it because I have invariably found that the ultimate roots of spiritual powerlessness in my ministry lay in my own life, and I may be pardoned if I think that there are many other men who are like myself. I am critical of the realized actualities because I believe so passionately in our unrealized possibilities. I am utterly convinced that the world wants a spiritual revival, and that the Church is not at present able to provide it, and that the Holy Spirit of God must sweep us again with His fire of light and power and joy before we can move forward from where we are.

Printed in the United States of America

ABOUT HEALING-HABITS

The classic spiritual texts republished by healing-habits
represent the rebirth of important books that had a significant
impact on the lives of the people of yesteryear. This is our
humble attempt to contribute, in a small way, to the healing
and recovery of people who are today suffering from any
malady of the body, mind, or spirit. The saving of even one
life makes our republishing worthwhile.

BOOKS REPUBLISHED BY HEALING-HABITS:

When Man Listens: Everyone Can Listen to God
by Cecil Rose; republished by Tuchy Palmieri
(BookSurge, 2008)

The Genius of Fellowship – Originally titled, **The Conversion of the Church**
by Samuel M. Shoemaker; republished by Tuchy Palmieri
(BookSurge, 2008)

Life Changers: 13th Edition
by Harold Begbie; republished by Tuchy Palmieri
(BookSurge, 2009)

Twice Born Ministers: We Are All Ministers
by Samuel M. Shoemaker; republished by Tuchy Palmieri
(BookSurge, 2009)

Children of the Second Birth
by Samuel M. Shoemaker; republished by Tuchy Palmieri
(BookSurge, 2009)

Twice Born Men: A Clinic of Regeneration
by Harold Begbie; republished by Tuchy Palmieri
(BookSurge, 2009)

ALSO BY CARL "TUCHY" PALMIERI – BOOKS ON RECOVERY

The Platinum Rule and Other Contrarian Sayings: The First 60 Years
(BookSurge, 2006)

Tuchy's Law and Other Contrarian Quotes To Help You In Life's Journey
(BookSurge, 2007)

Off The Wall Contrarian Quotes For People In Recovery
(BookSurge, 2007)

The Food Contrarian: Quotes for People Recovering From or Dealing With Eating Issues
(BookSurge, 2007)

Relationship Recovery: Healing One Relationship At A Time
(BookSurge, 2008)

ALSO BY CARL "TUCHY" PALMIERI – INSPIRATIONAL BOOKS

The Godsons: The Trinity Alliance
(BookSurge, 2007)

Josephine, In Her Words: Our Mom
(BookSurge, 2007)

Phil, In His Words: Our Dad
(BookSurge, 2007)

Relationship Magic
(BookSurge, 2008)

Money And So Much More: The True Meaning of Wealth
(BookSurge, 2008)

Sex and Intimacy: The Gifts of Life
(BookSurge, 2008)

Oprah, In Her Words: Our American Princess
(BookSurge, 2008)

Satisfying Success: And the Ways to Achieve It
(BookSurge, 2009)

Obama, In His Own Words: Pre-Election
(BookSurge, 2009)

ABOUT THE AUTHOR

Carl "Tuchy" Palmieri was born in 1942 in an old mansion belonging to the former mill owner of the factory where his father worked. His family was one of six related families that occupied the mansion. The second son of Italian immigrants, Carl grew up in Westport, Connecticut. After receiving a bachelor's degree in business administration from the University of Bridgeport he began his career marketing and installing accounting computers for the Burroughs Corporation. Twenty-one years later, in 1987, he started his own computer business. Carl is also the author of a series of self-help books.

Today Carl lives with his wife, Susan, in Fairfield, Connecticut. He has three children, two stepchildren, and 12 grandchildren. His nickname, Tuchy, comes from having been one of three Carls in his family. There was a "Big Carl," a "Carl the Twin," and "Carluch," which meant "Little Carl." "Carluch" evolved into "Carlatuch," "Tuch," and finally, "Tuchy."

Made in the USA
Charleston, SC
10 December 2010